BOYLAND

*A B.A.B.E.'s Guide
to Understanding Guys*

andrea stephens

Revell
Grand Rapids, Michigan

Published by Fleming H. Revell
a division of Baker Publishing Group
P.O. Box 6287, Grand Rapids, MI 49516-6287
www.revellbooks.com

Printed in the United States of America

Library of Congress Cataloging-in-Publication Data
Stephens, Andrea.
      Boyland : a B.A.B.E.'s guide to understanding guys / Andrea Stephens.
          p.   cm. (A B.A.B.E. book)
      ISBN 0-8007-5952-4 (pbk.)
          1. Teenage girls—Religious life. 2. Sex differences (Psychology)—
Religious aspects—Christianity. 3. Teenage boys—Psychology. I. Title
      BV4551.3.S733 2006
      248.8′33—dc22   2005028117

Portions of this book were previously published on www.andreastephens.com, in *Brio* magazine, and in the *B.A.B.E. MiniMag*.

Published in association with the literary agency of Alive Communications, Inc., 7680 Goddard Street, Suite 200, Colorado Springs, CO 80920.

interior design by brian brunsting

To Dad, R. J. Ardner,
the man who gave me my first glimpse
into the workings of the heart
and mind of the male gender.
You've modeled true love
in the way you've faithfully
loved Mom and held her in high esteem.
I'm blessed to be your daughter.

Inside BOYLAND

HOW COOL OF YOU!

It's thank-you time. I must start with my patient and kind editors, Jennifer Leep and Kelley Meyne. Thanks for extending grace (and deadlines) when I suddenly found myself overscheduled and moving across the country. I appreciate each of you.

Thanks to my *Brio* girls (and my friends) Lisa Velthouse, Natalie Lloyd, Andrea Taylor, and Katie Koerton, who contributed special sections for this book, sharing fun advice as well as pieces of their hearts for the sake of helping teen girls. You rock.

Special thanks to Pam Farrel and Michelle McKinney Hammond for sharing your expertise with young women who want to grow in their understanding of guys and life.

I got the best help from the coolest guys ever: Cody R., Cullen O., Jordan O., Drew H., Ryan H., Daniel B., Greg D., Adam K., David O., and Ryan W.! Thanks for letting me pick your brains about why guys do the things they do! (And why they wear boxers.)

Francie George and Suzette Rowland, thanks for being my five-alarm research angels. You're both divine friends.

Thanks to Pat Ericson for graciously allowing me to hide away in your Quail Valley B & B. I need peace and quiet when I write, and you made that possible.

A big thanks to Debbie Ulrich, Carol Donati, Leslie Ooms, Barbra Minar, Lana Crowel, Alisa Roberts, Carla O'Brien, and the other women I casually questioned about their sons. Your insight was priceless.

Thanks to Mom, Dad, and Nell—the best parents and mother-in-law a girl could ask for! I can't thank you enough for being here, bubble-wrapping my breakables, packing boxes better than the professionals, preparing the London B.A.B.E. Seminar supplies, and baking me chocolate oaties when I needed brain food (okay, sugar!). I may have never finished this book, the website, and everything else without you!

And Bill, the ultimate guy's guy, who educated this ultimate girl's girl on the ways of the opposite sex, thanks for toughing it out our first year of marriage while you endured outbursts like, "That was gross!" "Stop burping!" "Don't jab me—that's not nice!" "What's wrong with your brain?" "Quit—I hate to wrestle—please, not the pretzel thing again!" I'll stop there. You're my favorite!

Lord Jesus, will you kindly enrich the lives of each of these precious ones who have graciously enriched mine? Bless them a hundredfold for the patience, time, and energy they put into this project. In your holy name I pray. Amen! ●

The
B.A.B.E. JOURNEY

Once upon a time, there was a small-town girl who grew up loving fashion, makeup, and glittery jewelry. As a teen she had starstruck eyes! She wanted to be either Miss America or on the cover of *Vogue*!

Okay, this isn't really a fairy tale. It's my life.

I wanted the lights, the lenses, and the limos! I went for the pageant thing first. I polished up my guitar performance, improved my grades, read up on current events, and entered the Junior Miss Scholarship Program. I finished second in the state pageant. A few years later, I entered the Miss Oklahoma Pageant. Second again! Therefore, not being a state winner with obligations, I switched gears and prepared for a modeling convention scheduled for later that summer. Well, the Miss America dream was put on hold because the trip to New York City won me a contract with Wilhelmina Models, Inc.

I was thrilled. I packed my bags and moved to the city a few weeks later.

I was ready. I settled into a small apartment with several other models, then took to the streets for my go-sees (that's model talk for the word *interview*—you'd go see if you were the right person for the job) and photo shoots.

Lights, Camera . . . Critisicm?

I learned quite quickly that ad agents and photographers have no problem telling you if they don't like your appearance. "We're searching for someone with a different look." Or "The end of your nose is too rounded." Or "We don't like the way your neck curves." Or "Your teeth are too big." Really, nothing is off-limits for these people!

After a while, I noticed I started to be unsure of myself. It seemed my confidence was slipping away. Questions surfaced. Is this shirt right for me? Is my rear getting big? Does my makeup look good? Is my hair hip enough? Why would anyone want to hire me? Should I get this mole on my cheek removed? Do I have enough money for breast implants?

Even though in the short time I'd been in New York I'd landed a national commercial, been on several smaller magazine covers, and appeared in some catalogs, it wasn't enough to offset the negative comments and the comparisons. My sensitive nature soaked them right in. I felt that almost everything about me was wrong. Inadequate. Not good enough.

What Was God Up To?

At the same time, God was using my modeling experience to show me that he had a different plan for my life, a plan that would amount to more than just having my smiling face promoting a product or gracing a magazine cover. This was something that would be much bigger than being a supermodel or an A-list actress. It would be a plan that would have heart—his heart!

It was time to move home.

Yet it seemed to be the worst possible timing. I had just finished my composite card, and I was about to be officially introduced to the market in the Wilhelmina head book.

My roommates thought I was delirious.

"What could be more important than attaining superstar status or making some big bucks?" they argued. "Besides, you're signed with a great agency, you're working with a famous acting coach, and your vocal trainer's the best." They almost had me convinced. But as I watched one light up a joint, one mix a drink, and one pop her birth control pill, it just confirmed my inner conviction that God had something better for me.

A *Real* B.A.B.E.!

The second week after I moved home, I was handed information about a one-year Bible training program. I knew it was for me. Though I'd been a believer since I was young, I'd never really studied God's Word. In fact, I didn't get my first Bible until I was sixteen. Since my future was going to be about God's plans for me, knowing his Word was core. Yet little did I know that this would change my life most dramatically.

As I studied the Bible, I discovered many verses that explained God's view and opinion of me. I found out he created and designed me in a way that delighted him. To him, I was **beautiful**. I learned that I didn't have to look or act perfect for him to love me. He **accepted** me. And he gave me talents and spiritual gifts that he wanted me to develop so I could use them to serve him. I am **blessed** by him. And about that plan I mentioned earlier, it was starting to play out before my eyes. No flashy stuff that was here today and gone tomorrow. God's plan for me is **eternally significant**. From God's perfect perspective, I was a B.A.B.E—not a sexy, flirty chick in a short skirt and a low-cut top who wanted all the guys to like her, but a *real* B.A.B.E.: beautiful, accepted, blessed, eternally significant! And it's *his* perspective and opinion that matter!

See, he had to heal my self-esteem with the truth of his Word before he could use me to help heal yours. Many of the experiences God has taken me through have been part of his preparation to bring me to this point right now.

For Such a Time as This

These truths have lived in my heart for years, but God has brought them together under the acronym B.A.B.E. for such a time as this. My young friend, I have seen your generation struggle with depression, eating disorders, cutting, alcohol and drug addiction, casual sex, and hopelessness. I believe these are all symptoms of low self-esteem. They're holding many young women back from becoming all God has meant for them to be.

Well, not anymore.

Life will change when you finally see yourself the way God sees you. It's my life mission to help teen girls (and women) get a new perspective on life, on themselves, on God. I'm so blessed to be able to invest my life in the lives of God's girls through writing, speaking, and mission trips.

To every person who reads this, you are a B.A.B.E.! I prove it to you in the first book of the B.A.B.E. Book series, *Girlfriend, You Are a B.A.B.E.!* It's not based on feelings or social standards. It's based on the unchanging truth in God's Word.

So if you don't have a copy of the book, order one today right off my website at www.andreastephens.com or from the publisher at www.revellbooks.com and get started!

Oh, by the way. God calls us to imitate Jesus. So I am (and so are you) a model! Just a different kind. Isn't God cool? ●

"'For I know the plans I have for you,' declares the Lord, 'plans to prosper you and not to harm you, plans to give you hope and a future.'" Jeremiah 29:11 NIV

WHAT IS a B.A.B.E.?

B Is for Beautiful!

You're a divine diva! You're fearfully and wonderfully made—created by God himself! You're a work of art and were not haphazardly thrown together! You were in God's care before you were even born! You were his idea! God thinks you're outrageously gorgeous! God sends his Spirit to live within you to make you beautiful on the inside. You have God-Beauty!

A Is for Accepted!

You're unconditionally loved and accepted by God! You've already won his approval! He's your audience of One! He stands to applaud you because he's proud of you! You belong to God! You're forgiven. You don't need to seek the acceptance of others—you're number one with God. He thinks you rock! Ultimately, what God thinks is all that matters!

B Is for Blessed!

You're the privileged recipient of so many blessings straight from the heart of God! You have blessings no one can take away from you. You have special abilities—tons of talents! As a child of God, you're showered with spiritual blessings like salvation, forgiveness, eternal life, the Holy Spirit, and grace! You've been given spiritual gifts like leadership or encouragement or service! You're so blessed!

E Is for Eternally Significant!

You're here *on* purpose and *for* a purpose! God has a plan for your life! A plan that will bring you true meaning, fulfillment, and satisfaction! A plan that will put to use your special abilities and your spiritual gifts. A plan that will make a difference in the lives of others and in the kingdom of God. It's an eternally significant plan! You matter! ●

Girlfriend, you are a B.A.B.E.!

True CONFESSIONS

Okay, I admit to having moments in my life when I've been clueless about the male species. I grew up in a predominately female household—me, my two sisters, my mom, my dog Mitzi, and the odd man out, my dad. There was lots of talk about who would be the first one to need a bra, who had the grossest zits, who swiped the curling iron, and exactly how a tampon worked. Just the regular X-chromosome conversations. Beyond that, we were all into music, voice lessons, dance class, marching band, cheerleading, sewing (I made a ton of my own clothes so I never looked exactly like anyone else), chores, and seeing who could make the best Christmas cookies or come closest to duplicating Grandma Ardner's pancakes (she fried them in bacon grease and made her own brown-sugar-and-butter syrup that was worth every single calorie).

Sure, I was around guys at school, church, and ski club. Of course I loved going to football and basketball games to rate how the players looked in their uniforms—oops, I mean, to watch the burly boys run in a touchdown pass or execute the perfect layup shot. Okay, since I'm confessing stuff, I preferred the social aspects of the whole game thing to actually watching the sport in progress. Sometimes I was way more into what I was wearing, who was looking at me and my friends, who was with who, and whether or not the cheerleaders would mess up. Unfortunately, I never did understand all the plays and penalties for football—or any other sport, for that matter. I'm proud to say that I have slightly redeemed myself since those early days.

Needless to say, I had limited exposure to the ins and outs of the male gender. My friends who had brothers had a big advantage over me as far as being exposed to the quirks and oddities of guys. They knew that guys played rough and got great joy out of gross insects. And, of course, they knew that bodily noises were guys' favorite pastime. Yep, some girls knew more about guys than I did.

But that didn't mean they understood them.

I mean, really, who can truly understand these creatures who mumble a limited number of words per day, hate to spill their feelings, would rather go on a campout than to prom, and think nothing of ditching their current girlfriend to ask out her best friend?

Who really gets guys? God does. He's responsible for creating them in the first place. Hard to imagine, huh? However, God does everything *on* purpose and *for* a purpose. This is the exact reason we're going to go to him to get a better understanding of his numero uno human creation: man!

We'll journey together into Boyland with God as our leader, the Holy Spirit as our guide, and the Bible as our map. Our goal is to see why and how God designed guys differently than he designed us B.A.B.E.s. Then I'll introduce you to some great tools, like a personality test, and concepts, like birth order and layers of communication. You can gain useful insight that can be applied ASAP in your guy relationships. Then we'll get to the friendship versus dating thing.

Scattered throughout the pages, you'll read some Love Letters written from real dads to their daughters, expert insights from Christian leaders, and lots of ideas for creating memorable hang time with groups of your guy and girl friends, called Coed Craziness.

I promise this book (and lots of prayer!) will help you through the Boyland journey. ●

Warning! The spiritual general has determined the contents of this book may be hazardous to your current view on boys; precautions should be taken or else you risk the annihilation of all preconceived notions and untested theories, which will result in the formation of new, accurate, and thrilling information based on time-tested principles from "the book" (also known as the Bible) and professional boyologists.

Note: The contents herein are not about improving your dating status or how to find Mr. Right; they're not about being dateable or kissing anything good-bye; there is no dirt on sex. They are, however, packed with powerful tools and solid information that will rock your relationships.

Consider yourself warned.
Proceed at Your Own Risk!

Welcome to
BOYLAND

The Land Flowing with Milk and . . .
Cheeseburgers?

In a not-so-far-away place, beyond tall gates made of crushed soda cans, there exists a testosterone-filled territory with rugged terrain.

> It's a place where the climate can change continually but is rarely noticed.

> It's a place of baseball fields, soccer fields, football fields, and paintball fields.

> It's a place with skate ramps and trails for hiking and biking.

> It's a place with mega-size flat-screen TVs—all connected, creating the largest Xbox network ever!

> It's a place scented with smelly socks and sweaty jocks.

> It's a place where disputes are settled with rock-paper-scissors or a drag race.

> It's a place with rock and Bach, saxophones and cell phones.

It's a place with mega munchies—chili cheese fries to fried chicken to Chinese.

It's a place inhabited by boisterous and bashful beings whom God actually takes responsibility for creating!

It's a place that flashes a neon sign proclaiming, "Beware! You are now entering the Y-ChromoZone!™"

It's a place called . . . **Boyland**!

Boyland. Exactly who inhabits this land? It's those of the male persuasion who can sometimes **drive us crazy**! Sometimes they make us **feel like princesses**! Sometimes they **make us so mad**! And sometimes they can **melt our heart**s with one little grin!

Who am I referring to? You guessed it—**guys**!

B.A.B.E., give your head a quick shake, clear your mind, and focus in. You really, really, really want to hear and absorb this. Ready? Here goes.

Boyland and the Promised Land are absolutely, no way, not even a teensy bit close to being the same thing! The only thing they have in common is that they both end with the word *land*! In the Old Testament, God promised the Israelites that the special place where he was leading them would be a land flowing with milk and honey. That sounded glorious to them after years of eating boring, tasteless manna. Imagine how they daydreamed of freshly baked breads, juicy fruit right off the trees, roasted lamb chops. Oh, and yes, milk and honey!

Boyland, my friend, is a different story. Milk? Yes. Honey? Not so much.

The idea of milk and honey was more than just the actual milk and honey. It was the idea of a place that would be beautiful and fruitful and prosperous. It would be a land of peace and joy and real living. For the Israelites, the Promised Land indeed held great . . . well, um . . . promise!

Let me break it to you gently. The place you've been daydreaming of, the land that has fields of colorful flowers and heavenly scents, the place where guys stop and stare as you stroll the streets, the land where a special someone brings you roses and boxes of chocolate, the place with spas, salons, and shoe stores on every corner—that place doesn't exist. That would be called Girl-land. Boyland is a whole different story.

And the inhabitants are a whole different creature.

God's the one who created them. He's the one who scooped together a pile of dirt, formed it, then called it a man—Adam, to be exact. (That dirt thing, it explains a lot, doesn't it?) If I were God, I may have pleaded temporary insanity. But no. God stepped back, looked at his brand-new, one-of-a-kind design, and said, "It is good."

God was pleased, maybe even sorta proud of himself. This new species that was made in his very image would be able to walk and talk with him. It would be his friend. (Okay, that part kinda went haywire when Eve bit the forbidden fruit, but you get the gist of it, right?) What I'm saying is this: God created guys *on* purpose and *for* a purpose! (If you've read *Girlfriend, You Are a B.A.B.E.!* you knew this purpose stuff applied to you, but here it is in black and white—God was just as purposeful in the creation of guys.) God knew exactly what he was doing and why he was doing it. That may be a bunch to swallow.

Nevertheless, you're here. This is Boyland. Welcome.

So Why Are We Here?

Why have we ventured into Boyland? Because, as you may have noticed on your very first step through the crushed-can gates, this place is unique—borderline freaky in some girls' opinion. You and your friends may have entered Boyland a while ago, but if you're like most girls, there are times you get overwhelmed, weirded out, confused, maybe even totally lost! Times when you just have to stop and scream, "I don't understand guys!" Boyland isn't like the world you and your girlfriends live in. So think of the stuff on these pages as a map or a decoder! It's a necessity, since Boyland has its own set of road signs, rules, and ways of doing things. It's foreign to the typical girl. But a B.A.B.E. like you can't stay confused about guys, nor can you stay in the shelter of Girl-land; you have to venture out—will *want* to venture out. So think of our time together as signing up for lessons on how to navigate your way through this testosterone territory. You'll gain information and insight, wisdom and ways to deal, but most important, you'll grow in your understanding of this special gender!

Ultimately, a better understanding of guys helps you let them be who they are! Be who they are. Be who they are. Be who they are. Get the point? See, there are going to be things about guys that you just love. But there are also going to be some things you just won't! This will create times when you'll want to squeeze a poor unsuspecting male into *your* mold. If you see results, they'll be temporary. Ultimately, it's not going to happen.

You'll think you can change a guy (for the better, of course).

You'll think you can fix him (because girls know best, right?).

You'll courageously take him on like a project (forgetting that he's a fallen human being).

You'll try to please him to coax him to change (so exhausting!).

And let me clue you in on the outcome: you'll tear out your hair, chew off every last fingernail, weep with frustration, and spend hours on the phone with your friends, plotting and strategizing until your head wants to pop! And it will be pointless. Such a waste of precious time and brain cells.

Your greatest challenge as a female, as a B.A.B.E., as a sister, as a future wife, is to learn to understand this God-selected gender. No, of course you won't understand *everything*! There are sure to be times when you'll just have to shake your head and walk away.

Ultimately, understanding them will help you "allow" for the males God puts in your life. You know, just let them be themselves

A guy doesn't need your permission to be himself. He's got God's!

and like them anyway. It's giving them unspoken permission to be who they are. Note that I said *unspoken*. I don't suggest blurting out, "You are an oddity, but I'm going to give you permission to be that way."

No, granting them permission to be themselves isn't for them, it's really for *you*!

It brings a sense of calm to your churning insides. It brings peace to your puzzled mind. It brings ease to your embarrassment. And it all starts with an effort to understand them. And understanding brings acceptance. And acceptance opens the door to some fantastic friendships, and one day romance, with these Boylanders.

The Y Factor

A B.A.B.E. biology review:

There's an exquisite egg. There's a stud-muffin sperm. Each of them enters the runway of life bringing twenty-three miniscule things called chromosomes. One of these chromosomes determines sex—this gender-defining wonder is available in two styles, X and Y. Eggs always sport the finest of X fashion. Sperm, being more complex creatures, show up in either Y or X fashion.

If the exquisite egg struts down the runway with an X stud-muffin sperm, together they create an incredible new look called female. If, however, the exquisite egg is choreographed with the Y stud-muffin sperm, a whole different animal is created. Male. And it's all because of the Y.

Programmed into the Y chromosome is a plan to develop certain hormones in guys (girls aren't the only ones with hormones). The main hormone, testosterone—we'll call him Terone for short—is for developing a guy's maleness. Terone gushes four times his normal amount at two important times in a guy's life. First, when he's just a bundle of cells—about the sixth week of embryonic development. At this point, Terone causes the formation of male body parts and structures the brain to be male. Did you catch that? The male brain

get more of it in the books I used, like *Raising Sons and Loving It* by Gary and Carrie Oliver and *The Wonder of Girls* and *The Wonder of Boys* by Michael Gurian.

is structured and designed *differently* than the female brain is. This is absolutely key in your understanding of guys! Typically, the analytical left side of a guy's brain is larger and more highly developed than the creative, touchy-feely right side. This means a guy will tend to use the left side of his brain way more than the right. Here's another difference: the corpus callosum, which has a threadlike appearance, connects the two halves of the brain, or hemispheres, together. God has given guys less corpus callosum than he's given girls. This affects the way the right and left hemispheres of a guy's brain communicate with each other. So the two sides of his brain don't talk to each other the same way or the same amount that the two sides of a girl's brain do.

The second mega surge Terone is totally responsible for occurs at puberty, when he instructs the guy's bod to plunge forward into full manhood. During this time, not only do a guy's sexual organs fully develop, but he starts growing hair in various places, his voice cracks and squeaks as it becomes deeper, his sweat glands activate (enter acne and odor), and he appears to be living in a fog. Guys can get moody, angry, aggressive, and flighty. Dig it. Guys have their own form of PMS: pretty moody stud! But that's only when they're awake. The developing teen years are when guys love to sleep! And eat! Bottomless pits, they are (best said with a Yoda accent)!

So the Y factor, which brings Terone into a guy's life, is what makes a guy a guy! That's exactly the way it's supposed to be. Bottom line, God purposely chose to make males and females differently.

You'll never get any one guy totally figured out. So stop thinking you will. You won't.

The Guy Thing Is a God Thing

Since God is the one who designed the male and female body and brain, we can conclude that the guy thing is a God thing. It was part of his master plan for guys and girls to be completely different. The obvious conclusion we draw from studying the evidence is that guys are totally opposite of girls. Yes, guys and girls both have two legs, two feet, two arms, two hands, two eyes, two ears (this is starting to sound like a Noah's ark thing), but the similarities are limited. The bottom line is that God made guys, he made them the opposite of girls, and he did it on purpose!

Shocking, huh? But let's give him the benefit of the doubt; he is, after all, God.

Even our childhood nursery rhymes speak to the opposite nature of the sexes.

Sugar and spice
And everything nice.
That's what little girls are made of.
Snakes and snails
And puppy dog tails.
That's what little boys are made of.

Catch the chasm between the sexes. Girls are all about sweetness (until puberty hits!). Guys are all about slithering snakes, slimy slugs, and dog parts. Not very appealing but mostly true. Even when they're just little tikes, boys can be seen in rough-and-tumble play. They chase, tackle, kick, and pinch. They use all the space that's available to them. They prefer trucks instead of tea sets, squishing a bug instead of setting it free, and loud vroom-vroom noises instead of little giggles.

Opposites! And it never changes. Oh sure, you'll meet a few guys who are disgusted by burly belches and a few girls who can kick booty better than most guys, but generally speaking . . . opposites!

Here's some more evidence. I asked four guys and four girls the same questions. This is how they answered:

What's your favorite book?

Guys: *Series of Unfortunate Events: The Carnivorous Carnival*
Holes
1984
Purpose-Driven Life

Girls: *Little Women*
As You Like It
A Year and a Day
Shogun

What's the best movie you've seen in the last six months?

Guys: *Star Wars Episode III: Revenge of the Sith*
Batman Begins
The Longest Yard
Lord of the Rings

Girls: *The Land Before Time*
Boogeyman
The Notebook
The Sisterhood of the Traveling Pants

Name two items you couldn't live without.

Guys: fishing pole and a football
bathing suit and a skateboard
IPOD and truck
shorts and The Message

Girls: cell phone and shaving razor
Internet to IM my friends and clothes
eyeliner and Bible
yogurt and the laptop

What do you think would be a cool gift for a girl?

Guys: a bag of her favorite candy
       tickets to the rodeo
       I'm clueless
       something that makes her laugh

Girls: an outfit
       a gift certificate for a manicure
       a cool beach towel
       perfume

What's your favorite way to spend a Saturday afternoon?

Guys: playing football or basketball with friends
       playing video games
       paintball wars or fishing
       girl watching or sleeping

Girls: seeing a movie with friends
       taking a bubble bath and listening to relaxing music
       playing softball
       Murder Mystery party with friends

What do you want for Christmas this year?

Guys: video games
       paintball gun
       scuba equipment
       hunting boots

Girls: motorized scooter
       highlights
       a gift card for the mall
       cozy pajamas

See? Opposites. In fact, to some degree, guys are opposite girls in almost every way—down to the last cell! The way they think, the things they feel, the build of their bodies, the whole idea of sex, the way they relate to God, and even the way they shop!

Okay, *technically* speaking, guys and girls aren't 100 percent different—we already went over the ten fingers and ten toes thing. But that may be where it ends! Guys and girls even grow and mature at different rates. Generally, girls mature faster than guys—about two years sooner. That accounts for some of the differences between the sexes. The rest of the differences can be attributed to the divine plan.

Understand Them? Why Try?

The logical question is, If guys are so incredibly different from us girls, why even try to understand them? Why waste our time?

Because they're *everywhere*! It's not even remotely possible that you won't see them, hear them, or smell them (crude as it is, that's a fact). And there's an 88.8 percent chance that you'll end up married to one of them.

This is one of those times when I'm grateful that the Bible explains to us that God's thoughts are higher than ours and his ways are higher than ours (Isaiah 55:9). Here we are thinking it might be a frustrating and impossible feat to figure out these creatures. But God doesn't see it from our perspective. See, since his plan is for one man and one woman to join together in marriage and then live together as husband and wife forever and ever and ever, God thinks it would be an awesomely advantageous thing for us girls to at least attempt to understand guys, to try to decode them.

"We can't stand it when girls act stupid and they think it's cute, or when they're indecisive and moody without *any* warning, or when they point out your flaws, or when they forget they're in public and chew like camels."
Drew, Ryan, Michael

News flash: Guys definitely don't have the decoding details on us divine divas! In other words, they don't understand girls!

Okay, that makes sense, right? Truly, God's perspective always makes sense.

Though it's impossible to completely understand a guy (be it your dad, brother, or friend), it's something we are to pursue. To *understand* means to be able to comprehend or identify with another person. It's a sense of knowing something on a deep level or grasping the meaning. It's when you say, "Oh, I get it!"

Understanding also implies seeing something from that person's point of view or empathizing—feeling something that person feels. No doubt, this takes effort. All relationships take effort. When you get a glimpse into the character and nature of guys, you'll be doing yourself a great favor. You'll be setting yourself up for more meaningful friendships, which will enrich your life. I'm not talking about dating, like when your romantic emotions start messing with your head and your heart. I'm talking about appreciating guys for who they are and how friendship with them can add balance to your life. Besides, statistics prove that long-lasting love relationships start with solid friendships.

I had dinner with singer Natalie Grant and her hubby, Bernie, while on a mission trip to Ecuador. Natalie had been badly hurt in a "young love" relationship and wasn't looking for love. Bernie was an extremely talented musician, and that common interest sparked a friendship. They spent two years being good friends, getting to know each other for who they were on the inside—their thoughts, hopes, and dreams—before their first date! They've now been happily married for years. How cool is that?

Attempting to understand the way a guy thinks (mental), feels (emotional), is built (physical), relates to God (spiritual), and even **shops** will enrich your life and your relationships. This is worth investigating. Time to dig in so we can get the full dish in each of these five areas. Let's take a look. ●

"Girls should understand and accept the fact that guys can be dumb, so we need them to talk openly. Be frank and direct. And please, don't speak in code language. We don't get it." Tim, 16

"It's a turnoff when girls act all stupid when really they aren't." Brian, 15

"Guys like girls who can relax around them and laugh normally." Joshua, 13

OBVIOUS OPPOSITES

Knock Knock, ANYBODY THERE?

Understanding Mental Differences

"What's wrong with his brain?" "What was he thinking?" "Does that guy even have a clue?" Admit it. These questions—and others like them—have darted through your thoughts, and probably more than once! Connecting brain to brain is a huge challenge in guy-girl friendships. Part of the reason for this is that guys' brains are different from ours. We already know that our brains develop differently, the left side of a guy's brain is larger than a girl's, and a girl has more corpus callosum, which allows for more interaction between the two hemispheres of the brain. Girls are working off both sides of the brain to a greater degree, so we tend to look at a situation from many different angles. We can see it this way and that way, and we're full of what ifs! (Add our emotions to the mix, and it really complicates stuff—no wonder it can take us *forever* to make decisions sometimes!)

Let's take a look at the basic mental differences between the sexes.

Guys . . .

- tend to be thinkers, not feelers (our society encourages this)
- are into analyzing everything (figure it out and forget about it)
- tend to be goal oriented
- can forget to use common sense
- tend to give their full attention to a single task/person at a time
- like to get things done
- are quick problem solvers
- are best at focusing on one thing time at a time (they're waffle heads—more on this later)
- don't like to ask for directions (they're famous for this)
- don't need to talk to the same girl every day (and it doesn't mean he's mad)

- are content to be silent and aren't big on talking—especially on the phone
- like games and activities with intense concentration (and rapid eye movement)

Girls . . .

- like to talk, talk, talk, talk, sleep, eat, then talk, talk, talk
- tend to feel first, think second
- often have keen insights, making them able to notice details and pick up on others' feelings
- enjoy the process of doing things,

"Sometimes when a girl asks me what I'm thinking about, I say 'nothing,' but that's not good enough. She assumes that I just don't want to tell her what I'm thinking about or that I'm hiding something, but no—I'm really *not* thinking about anything. Well, nothing specific. Girls shouldn't push and pry. Sometimes a guy likes being blank."
Christopher, 16

not just completing them (like scrapbooking—the joy is in the journey)

- can think about more than one thing at a time
- excel at multitasking (talking on the phone, listening to a CD, and painting their toenails all at the same time)
- tend to overthink situations and relationships
- have a greater need to understand things
- are glad to ask for directions (and arrive more quickly)
- may take longer to make decisions

Hints

- Never attempt a deep, meaningful conversation when a guy is watching football, listening for the fishing report, reading the newspaper, or lost in a PlayStation game.
- Stay true to your girl-like trait of looking at situations from various angles. Just don't beat it to death or you'll totally lose the guy's attention.
- Don't get offended if a guy isn't attentive on a consistent basis—his brain is just elsewhere, and he isn't ignoring you or sending an "I really don't like you" message.
- Going on a girl-guy trip? Look up the route on MapQuest so asking for directions isn't an issue.
- Don't assume guys are slow, dumb, or disinterested if they can't follow your fast-paced, topic-hopping conversation.
- Have close girlfriends! Girls *need* girlfriends. We have all those words to use on someone who can relate to what we're saying. My former youth group members Lily, Jordan, Alyson, and Ashley made a pact to hang on to their friend-

"Don't talk so much. You keep putting your foot in your mouth. Be sensible and turn off the flow!" Proverbs 10:19 TLB

ship through thick and thin and to *never* let a guy come between them. They went to church, school dances, concerts, mission trips, and even doctor's appointments together. Two of them have gone to the same college, and they've all traveled Europe together. When they're all coming into town for holidays, they rush to each other's houses to get the first hug. They're tight, bonded, forever friends.

Boy Bashing

Have you noticed it on TV? Do you catch it in song lyrics? Have you seen it on girls' T-shirts? "Boys are dumb." "Boys are stupid." "Girls rule!" "Let a woman do it!" While some of this seems humorous and causes us to snicker, the attitudes behind this kind of boy bashing can be harmful—to guys and to girls.

It's true that guys may not respond as quickly to the teacher's questions, they may not jump in to share their opinions in the middle of a hot debate, and they

might give you the blank stare when you ask about their feelings, but it's not because they're dumb, stupid, or empty headed! Their brains are different—God designed them that way. It isn't a girl's job to catch guys just being guys, then point it out, making them the target of laughter.

None of us wants to be laughed at or ridiculed. It feels awful. It makes us feel inadequate, like losers. Well, it affects guys the same way. They're not going to show their hurt right that second, but it's there. In fact, if it grows like a cancer, it can erupt in violence. Think of all the school shootings. Guys. Think of all the teens on death row. Guys. Think of all the adolescent suicides. Guys—mostly. When they're put down, made fun of, and belittled, it devalues them and crushes their self-esteem.

Jesus had a little something to say on this topic.

> "It really bugs me when a girl goes on and on and on and on talking about every little thing going on in her life. It makes me want to get away."
> Culver, 14

Coed Craziness

Take advantage of what you just learned about the mental differences in the sexes and try some games and activities you might both enjoy.

Puzzles and Popcorn! Choose some puzzles with guy-friendly subject matter (leave the kittens snuggled in a basket on the shelf), pop some extra-buttery microwave popcorn, and grab some sodas. Dump each puzzle on a separate table or place on the floor. Have at it! Guys will get to use their problem-solving brains and desire to complete things to get every last piece in place.

Scrabble Mania! This requires thought, concentration, and the know-how to spell. Set up the game and grab a dictionary in case your friends start making up words they swear are for real! You can expand this idea by making it a tournament of board games. Add Monopoly, Risk, chess—anything! Set it up as a competition!

PlayStation or Xbox Bash! Hook up enough TVs and control boxes to get a roar going. Just don't get frustrated if the guys take over the whole shebang.

Plane Party! Go to the craft store or the local library to get a book with illustrations on creating paper airplanes (or search it out online). Get various colors and sizes of the recommended type of paper. Challenge your friends to create the coolest plane, the longest-flying plane, the highest-flying plane, even the biggest dud plane. Have prizes ready for the winners.

Box Car Derby! Building can be a lesson in patience and teamwork. Unless you want to go for the real deal with wood, nails, and moveable parts, try this alternative. Ask your local furniture store, appliance center, or grocery store for all sizes of boxes (especially refrigerator and mattress boxes). Gather up scissors, box cutters, hot-glue guns, duct tape, and any creative items you can think of. Separate your friends into two or three coed teams. Let each team design and build a cardboard box car. When finished, ask parents or youth leaders to be the judges. Have a parade and see who wins!

It's known as the Golden Rule, but really it's the *Godly* Rule: Treat others the way you want to be treated (Matthew 7:12).

How are you supposed to treat others? _____

_____

_____

Do you do it?

Here are a couple more:

Everyone who is angry with his brother shall be guilty before the court; and whoever says to his brother, "You good-for-nothing," shall be guilty before the supreme court; and whoever says, "You fool," shall be guilty enough to go into the fiery hell.

Matthew 5:22 NASB

If you call your friend an idiot, you are in danger of being brought before the court. And if you curse him, you are in danger of the fires of hell.

Matthew 5:22 TLB

According to Jesus, is it okay to insult a guy's intelligence? Is it cool to call him a fool? And what about his physique or clothes or car or athletic skill? Do you have the go-ahead to slam him? No!

In other words, treat guys like they matter and like they have brains!

Since it comes from the God who made guys, the Lord who experienced ultimate ridicule and humiliation on the cross, I think we should take this instruction to heart. We can never know what another person has been through. Bashing someone makes us his judge—that's God's job.

So cut the remarks. Refuse to join in the verbal slams. Stop the gossip.

Champion a guy's person. Take his side. Respect him.

Be his real friend. And maybe even his hero. ●

HIDe-and-Seek
Understanding Emotional Differences

It's a brain thing again. God gave guys less of the hormone serotonin, which results in decreased emotional development in the brain. The left side of the male brain is smaller than the right side, and it's smaller than the left side of the female brain. Since guys' and girls' brains develop differently, that means they *are* different! A guy doesn't have the exact range of emotions a girl has. And this is a good thing! Think of how great it is that guys are *not* emotional maniacs. Temper tantrums, sob sessions, moodiness, all-out goofiness, and instant hyperability (that's not a real word) are all things that are pretty much reserved for us fascinating females. What a chaotic mess friendships and marriages would be if both genders excelled in emotions to the same depth. God is so smart. He wants relationships to work and for us to be compatible, so he put a different mix in the male and female formulas!

Now, that's not to say that guys don't have *any* emotions; they do! Ask them how their favorite team is doing—you'll see feelings. Ask them why they got grounded—you'll see feelings. Ask them if it was hard when their grandfather died—emotions will be right there. So understand that guys were created with emotions—they're different and less intense than ours. Your challenge as a friend is to discover the keys to drawing out those emotions. We'll dig into that later, but for now, take a look at the differences.

Guys . . .

- tend to be activity oriented (less emotion required)
- tend to stay bottled up inside
- need hard physical activity to release pent-up emotions
- often struggle to tell others how they feel
- are less likely to "stew" on issues—they let them go quickly
- are less sentimental about some of the things girls find sentimental
- are less attached to mementoes—they don't have special boxes under their beds with their dried-out prom boutonnières or ticket stubs from their fav movies
- can be uncomfortable with their feelings
- tend to be less in touch with their feelings
- are less aware of others' feelings; therefore, they don't connect well on an emotional level
- struggle with anger more than with other emotions
- hold fewer grudges
- are more likely to use alcohol, drugs, or sex to handle negative emotions
- may wrestle with depression (rates are increasing among guys)
- can feel used if girls take advantage of their friendliness

"It's hard to be vulnerable with girls. I took this girl I really liked to senior prom. We only danced the slow songs. I felt too embarrassed to tell her that I fast dance like a baboon; really, I just don't look cool. After that night, she never talked to me again."
Jeremy, 18

Girls . . .

- tend to be relationship oriented (more emotion required)
- love to express their feelings
- can be drama queens
- have several thousand more words to say in a day than guys do (this is documented truth)
- tend to exaggerate emotions
- are more likely to want everyone to know why they're upset
- can be moody
- tend to be sentimental (they have special boxes under their beds with dried corsages, hairs from a guy's sweater, etc.)
- can be grudge queens
- may allow too much talk to turn into gossip
- get depressed more easily than most guys
- like to change their minds based on their moods
- need to talk through problems and emotions
- often romanticize things and set themselves up for big letdowns

Most girls are all about feelings. "I'm so excited." "He really crushed me." "I'm really in the dumps today." "Gosh, I'm lonely." Feelings are part of who we are as divine divas—we were designed that way. We're blessed with more serotonin and female hormones (estrogen and progesterone) that can affect us that way. Notice how different the above list is from the guys' list you just read.

Hints

- Ask a guy how he *feels* about something and watch his eyes roll back in his head! Guys can freeze up with the *feel* word. Instead, ask them, "What do you *think* about . . ." They react better to the *think* word.

- Don't get overly introspective about everything. It may squeeze some of the joy out of your life.

- Beware of drawing the conclusion that a guy doesn't care about your problem just because he can't relate like your girlfriends can and just because he has nothing to say when you're done giving him every last detail!

- Welcome guys' emotional need (it's self-esteem related) to set and reach their goals.

- To help a guy friend get something off his chest, engage him in

"Here are ten things guys want girls to know:

1. Cut the drama.
2. Don't overanalyze.
3. Don't act mad just to get us to talk to you.
4. Drama queens don't get real guys.
5. Don't be hyperemotional.
6. Drama is a turnoff.
7. Don't tell us *everything* that happens in your life. We like our ears — don't talk them off!
8. No drama.
9. If we tell you something, don't blab it around the school or youth group.
10. Just say *no* to drama."

Ryan, 16

an athletic or mindless activity; then keep quiet when he starts to open up.

- Don't get your feelings hurt if your brother (a guy) doesn't keep that birthday gift you made him two years ago. He still loves *you*, but he's not emotionally attached to the gift.

- If you and a guy have a conflict that you stress over for days and days, don't be disappointed when you bring it up and he doesn't know what you're talking about.

Was Jesus a Girly Man?

Our society teaches guys that showing emotions like gentleness, sympathy, or even pain is a sign of weakness. It's that whole "big boys don't cry" thing. It's the belief that showing a softer side makes you a sissy. Uh-oh. If expressing emotions and showing a softer side makes a guy a sissy, then that would make Jesus a sissy! You won't catch *me* saying that to his face, especially since it's a lie!

The Bible shows us plenty of times when Jesus got emotional—both weepy and reckless. One of the obvious places Jesus got ticked off was in the temple.

> Jesus entered the temple area and drove out all who were buying and selling there. He overturned the tables of the money changers and the benches of those selling doves. "It is written," he said to them, "'My house will be called a house of prayer,' but you are making it a 'den of robbers.'"
>
> Matthew 21:12–13 NIV

That's what I would call angry, and rightfully so. But can he show the flipside of anger too and show love?

So the sisters sent word to Jesus, "Lord, the one you love is sick."

John 11:3 NIV

Mary and Martha knew that Jesus loved their brother, Lazarus, because they'd seen it in his actions. In due time, Jesus went to Lazarus and raised him from the dead!

Jesus felt very deeply. He wasn't afraid or ashamed to show his emotions. In John 11, the account of Lazarus's death, Jesus saw Mary, Martha, and many friends crying and wailing over the loss of Lazarus. Taking it all in, Jesus was overcome with grief. The Bible's shortest verse records what happened next:

Jesus wept.

John 11:35 NIV

People don't just make themselves cry real tears at the appropriate times so they look caring to others. Tears come from true emotion.

In another incident, Jesus's love and compassion are clearly demonstrated.

When He went ashore, He saw a large crowd, and felt compassion for them and healed their sick.

Matthew 14:14 NASB

One more example. Picture him hanging on the cross by three nails that were ripping through his flesh. Imagine his face so badly beaten and his body so badly thrashed by whips that he was unrecognizable. See his blood streaming from his open wounds. Now hear Jesus push out these words with the last bit of breath left inside him.

> Father, forgive them; for they do not know what they are doing.
>
> Luke 23:34 NASB

There was nothing sissy about that.

Jesus shows us that emotions from a male are part of who God has made him to be. No doubt there are good emotions and bad emotions, but when you see a guy expressing good and healthy emotions, encourage it. Don't laugh. Don't stare. Don't call him a baby or a girl.

It's scriptural fact that one of God's greatest goals for guys is for them to become like Jesus, to be "conformed to the likeness of his Son" (Romans 8:29 NIV). To help them do that, God gives them (and us) the Holy Spirit. Scripture is clear that when we confess our sinfulness, admit our need for God, and invite God's Son, Jesus, into our heart, making him our personal Savior and Lord, God sends the Holy Spirit to live *inside* us (John 14:17, 23; 1 Corinthians 3:16–17; 6:19). It's incredible. It's a miracle. It's a total God thing. Part of divinity comes to take up residence in every guy who calls Jesus Lord. And what's the eventual result of the Holy Spirit hanging out in that guy? Patience. Kindness. Gentleness. Love. Joyfulness. Peacefulness. Goodness. Faithfulness. Self-control (Galatians 5:22–23).

These are emotions! It's God's desire for guys to feel love, to feel joy, to feel peace, to feel kindness, and so on. This stuff is not for sissies, but for true men of God. ●

The Holy Spirit living *inside us* **turns ordinary girls into divine divas. He gives us our B.A.B.E. status! Get the complete dish on this in** *Girlfriend, You Are a B.A.B.E.!* **section 3, "B is for Blessed!"**

Love Letter—From the Heart of a Dad

Dear Bethany, Emily, and Rachel:

Some years back, Mom bought me three copies of a book to give to each of you girls at the appropriate time. The book is based on a song called "Butterfly Kisses." The book/song is about a father looking back, thinking about the relationship he had over the years with his daughter.

Well, the books are still sitting in my closet, and we're way beyond the years of butterfly kisses. We're also way beyond the years when boys thought girls were yucky. As you girls are blossoming into the beautiful young women you are, you'll notice more boys flitting around. Okay, Bethany and Emily are more aware, but soon, Rachel, when you come up for air from your gymnastics competitions, you'll notice too.

Anyway, I've noticed, and that's why I want to say something before that just gets left on a dark shelf somewhere as well. I love you and want to share my perspective on the guy-girl thing. This letter gives you the opportunity to simply take in what I want to say without feeling like you're getting preached to or lectured at.

Sexual purity is a joke in the world we live in today. People value instant gratification and treasure pleasure. I pray your sexual purity is precious to you, however. I want you to value your beauty—physical, sexual, and spiritual—as a wonderful gift from God. People

"For me to open up to a girl, she would have to show me that I can trust her, and show she has good opinions on life's problems." Michael, 17

"When a girl is genuine and I know she sincerely cares about me as a friend, then I'm more willing to let her know what's happening in my private life." Chris, 16

tend to look after and care for what they value and treasure. You will discover that if you wait until you are married to enjoy your sexuality in the way God intended, with whom God intended, you will know greater joy, peace, and contentment than those who pursue those things in the immediate gratification of their body's desires. How do I know? I had many friends—guys and girls—who gave it all away and regretted it. I also know because God promises us these things as well as warns us of what happens when we refuse to believe those promises.

What I want you to try to understand now is how sexual purity goes hand in hand with reputation (what you are known for). An old proverb says, "A good name is to be more desired than great riches; favor is better than silver or gold." The name and reputation you begin to establish now will have a great impact on the kind of guys who are attracted to you. The company you keep, the language you use, the clothes you wear, the activities you enjoy—all these things begin to establish your reputation. Take a look around. Do you know of any girls with the reputation for being sexually loose or easy? What kind of boy comes sniffing around them? On the flip side, what caliber of boys hang out with girls who have a reputation of being goody-goodies? There is a difference!

My own perspective is that during their teenage years, most guys live in a fog brought on by the changes in their bodies. They think about sex a lot more than you do and often view girls as objects designed to meet their needs more than as the truly beautiful people you are. If you're wise, you'll always think about motives when it comes to guys.

So I want you to keep control of the situation. I want you to set the boundaries based on whose you are (God's) and your own self-respect. One of the best boundaries you might want to draw throughout your high school years is to say, "I want to develop friendships with guys, not look for romance." Therefore, decide what kind of qualities you want in a guy friend before you even start to mess around with boyfriends and all the different pressures such a change in relationship suggests. Do you really want to hang out with guys who talk trash? Is a guy who presses you sexually or wants you to break away from all your other friends to spend time with just him really a friend?

Speaking of the company you keep, remember that you have each other as sisters. As sisters, you would do well to speak highly of and defend each other when you hear gossip or rumors about your sister. Moreover, why not develop your relationship, where you can share with someone you know is a sister in Christ as well as the sister across the hall who "won't let me wear her clothes"?

And finally, while you want everyone to speak well of you and defend your reputation, you're the one who carries the load. If people choose to speak maliciously against you because of your good behavior, then it is to their shame. If people speak poorly of you because of your questionable behavior, it is to your shame. The path to happiness is to set apart Christ as Lord in your heart.

I love you. I want you to come to me anytime to talk about sex, boys, whatever. I want you to know that if you're ever in a situation where you are not comfortable, you can call me night or day and I will come get you with no questions asked (for at least twenty-four hours).

Love,
Dad

"I sound corny saying this, but I want a girl to like me for my personality, not for my eyes or hair or rear end."
David, 14

THE BIG HUNT

Understanding Shopping Differences

Please sit down. Maybe you should lie down. The stuff I have to tell you might twist your brain and cause you to collapse. And it might happen more than this one time. The news break headed your way will affect you for your entire life. Therefore, I just had to put it in a category all its own.

Take a deep breath, hold it five seconds, blow it out. Better do it again.

Here it comes . . .

Guys don't like to shop.

There! I said it! Keep breathing, B.A.B.E! It will help. So will my explanation. Let's define the word *shop*. Webster's Dictionary says it means to diligently examine with the intent to purchase, to search the offerings of a store, to pursue, to research—these are all great shopping words! Girls are into tracking down what they want—or what they have in their mind's eye (we usually have an idea or feeling about what we're looking for, right?).

What guys do when they go to the mall or a store to buy clothes is nothing like this. In fact, what they do greatly resembles hunting. It's far more single focused than shopping. I've laid it out for you below.

Guys . . .

- go into one store (enter the field)
- locate the guys' department (locate their prey)
- approach one rack (sneak up on the poor unsuspecting animal)
- find one pair (watch out buddy, you're going down)
- take the one pair, from the one rack, from the one department, in the one store, to the one salesclerk (raise the gun; prepare to shoot)
- pay (bang)
- exit the store as fast as possible (drag the animal back to the truck, secure it, and peel out of the area)
- head to the food court to pig out (head home for lunch)

Girls . . .

- call all their friends to make arrangements when and where to meet (Go alone? No way!)
- visit no fewer than five stores—it's a law
- familiarize themselves with the style options—in various departments and in various stores
- research the price differences—a very admirable quality
- want to know the color choices—certain colors make them glow
- pursue the perfect purse to match—well, naturally
- search out matching earrings—duh
- want to find shoes to match—double duh
- go to the food court to rest and talk over their choices with their girlfriends—critical step
- find out if items are returnable—females reserve the right to change their minds
- make final purchases
- exit the mall with packages and still have a spring in their step

Hints

- If you know a guy who says "sweet" to going shopping with you, just know he isn't in it for the long haul.

- If you make a guy choose between going to the mall with you or watching the big playoff game, forget it. Don't make him choose. You'll be disappointed (the game will win).

- If a bunch of your friends (coed) are going to hit the stores, save yourself and the guys in the group some grief by planning ahead. Look at ads and make some calls. Know which stores you want to go to so you won't be such a looky-lou.

- If you accompany a guy to a store to hunt something down for him, keep it about him. When he's done, avoid dragging him all over. Honor his shopping style instead of making it about you.

- Don't jump-start his frustration level by bringing him other options to try on. The one he picked out is fine. Girls rarely want *fine*. They want cool.

So there you have it—the very opposite shopping styles of the sexes! ●

"Some of us guys
think and feel
things very
deeply, but we
don't know how
to get it from
our hearts to our
heads, then out
of our mouths."
B.J., 17

ABSOLUTE OPPOSITES

THE SAGA CONTINUES

Sorta Similar,
SORTA NOT
Understanding Physical Differences

Guys are sorta similar to girls in some ways. Yet the male physique is quite different from the female one. Guys are built to be workers; we're built to be nurturers—yes, even by body design, women are built to be mothers, to cuddle and care for the young. Yet both sexes struggle with body image due to our society's unrealistic body standards. We see computer-enhanced photos that make models and entertainers look hot. We start thinking that's what we need to look like to be considered attractive. Not possible—not for girls, not for guys. We girls forget that guys struggle with body image too. It's important that we remember for ourselves, but also for the guys in our lives, that God says that we're fearfully

"In tenth grade, I was only 5'2", my voice hadn't changed, and I couldn't develop muscles no matter how much I lifted. But I was fast. I made the JV football team, but that didn't stop people, especially girls, from calling me sucky names like 'peewee' or 'pretty boy.' I hated going to school, hated my body, and hated the girls who made fun of me."
Marcus, 18

and wonderfully made, that he knit us together in the design he desired. No matter what they look like, guys are handsome studs from God's perspective, just like you're beautiful in God's eyes. If a guy gets touchy when you tease him about his facial features or body, now you know why.

Check out the differences.

Guys . . .

- have testosterone as their main hormone (flashback from section 1)
- have longer vocal chords
- have thicker skin (physically and emotionally)
- have stronger and larger muscles
- generally have broader shoulders and chests
- grow more hair on their arms, legs, chest, belly, back, and face
- have extra body parts known as testicles (popularly known as "balls") and a penis (often referred to as a "weenie" or "sausage" or actually given a name!)
- struggle with body image (culture shows them tall, muscular men with hairy chests)
- experience voice changes (they're very sensitive about this—never tease them)
- play rougher, need more space, and like activities that use the whole body (like football or tennis)
- are usually quite competitive—they can turn anything into a game
- love physical activity, from paintball wars to jet skiing to wrestling anything in sight
- use physical activity to release pent-up energy or emotions—a great stress reducer
- take more physical risks and have the need for speed
- don't want to look like girly men
- like fast eye movement (they're easily addicted to video games, etc.)
- have a higher metabolism and can lose weight

faster—in fact, when they gain weight, it's around the belly, while girls gain weight around the rear and upper thighs

- might exchange a fist-to-fist touch or an easy smack, punch, or push with other guys as a way of expressing camaraderie

Girls . . .

- have estrogen and progesterone as their main horomones
- have girl parts: uterus, ovaries, fallopian tubes, cervix, clitoris, vagina, and breasts
- have a menstrual cycle (this typically ranges from twenty to twenty-eight days)
- have less hair on their bodies

- have wider hips (for birthin' babies within marriage!)
- are designed to be more fleshy around the waist, hips, and thighs (this does not mean girls are *fat*!)
- have a higher pain tolerance (good thing we pop out the babies)
- have softer skin (we're way more squeezable)
- use their shorter vocal chords a lot
- typically don't name their body parts

Are you keen to all this cool stuff about your *gorgeous* God-given bod?

Hints

- Never tease a guy about his body; he hates teasing as much as you do. If his voice cracks, his face is loaded with whiteheads,

Want to say "hey" or express your support for a guy? Limit physical touch to a light hit fist-to-fist, a mild punch on the upper arm, or a quick pat on the upper back. Forget the smack on the rear that we witness among male teammates—his bum is off-limits for you!

or his feet are huge, please refrain from laughter.

- Remember that guys have a testosterone surge from around age thirteen to sixteen, which may account for erratic behavior.
- Guys are less modest about their bodies.
- Because of their competitive nature, guys may try to be better than you. Don't take it personally. It's part of their wiring.
- If a guy gets physically injured but tries to act like it's no big deal, go ahead and still be compassionate, even baby him a bit. It makes him feel cared for.
- Never, under any circumstances, share names you might have for your body parts. You'll regret it if you do.
- Never, under any circumstances, ask a guy his name for his body parts. Very uncool!

I just have to tell you this. While I was in the process of writing this book, a little incident occurred that perfectly il-lustrates the first three categories of differences we've looked at. Get this. It's Saturday morning at 8:00, and I'm crossing the parking lot on my way to the church office building (where my husband is the pastor) when I run into Carrie (a recent high school grad).

"Hey, Carrie! What are you doing here so early?"

"I'm coaching a kids' soccer team, and we have a game at eight thirty—you should come!"

"Cool, I can do that. See you then."

Okay, so at 8:46 a.m., I wander over to the activities building as promised. On one end of the indoor soccer field, I see Carrie and her girlfriend Jordan, obviously co-coaches. Coaching the other team is Garreth, a college junior, who lives and breathes soccer. Garreth is leaning forward over the railing, shouting instructions and encouragement to his players. Carrie and Jordan are leaning up against the wall, deep in conversation. The kids play on. Fast forward to halftime. I noticed that none of Garreth's players were on the field. He had them huddled together as a team, focusing on the game at hand. Since guys are competitive, he was probably rearranging their strategy to ensure the victory. When the plan was finalized, Garreth took his team out on the field and personally challenged them to a game—him against all of them! Carrie and Jordan's players were on the field playing around with the ball. Their coaches were still doing what? *Talking!* After all, that's what girls do. See? Perfect, huh? I later learned that Garreth had no idea what color his team jerseys were and had no team name. The girls adored the electric blue shirts that made their team "pop," their team name was the Sharks, and when they scored a goal, the whole team was to clasp their hands together over their heads like a shark's jaw. Cute. Hand motions. The girls had hand motions. Believe me, that thought never crossed Garreth's mind. The girls were enjoying the process of the game, enjoying talking with the kids (probably not about soccer), and digging on the chance to talk to each other. ●

THE URGE TO MERGE
Understanding Sexual Differences

During a guy's teen years, the second jolt of testosterone strikes his system, and his body comes alive in a whole new way. He starts to be preoccupied with his new desires and urges. He's very aware of his body and all female bodies. He can't get this one thing off his mind. It's spelled *S-E-X*.

Add the fact that guys are wired to respond to what they see. They're visually stimulated. God made them that way. Put them in the school cafeteria with girls wearing midriffs, halter tops, or tight low-rise jeans, and their bodies start reacting. It's sorta automatic.

Let him watch an hour of TV, and he'll see tons of visual images that can take his brain to Sexville. Drop him off at the mall. All he has to do is walk past the window display at Victoria's Secret. Bam. Put him in front of a magazine rack in the grocery store. His eyes will keep wandering back to the very exposed cover girls (with the computer-enhanced boobs).

Then there's this thing called peer pressure. Guys say and do things to each other. Locker room stuff. They pry. Their inquiring minds want to know: have you had sex?

No? Why? Yes? With who? How many times? It all stinks. It's hard on guys. There aren't a ton of people encouraging them to stay virgins. There aren't many guys wearing purity rings.

And then there's the whole question of whether or not a guy is a man if he hasn't had sex (more on this coming up). Years ago it was about stealing a kiss or maybe a touch, but in our world today, it's more like, "Hi, I'm Sam." "I'm Sue." "Let's have sex!" It's very blatant—and not at all the beautiful, bonding experience God means for sex to be.

I'm sharing this because I want you to understand what's driving a guy's passions. None of this takes away his responsibility or ability to control his sexual urges. And it doesn't justify his actions if he goes out and has sex. But what guys are dealing with isn't the same thing girls are dealing with. It's been a known fact through the ages that guys are about sex and girls are about romance. We want a guy to bring us flowers, send us e-cards, and buy us gifts. Guys don't care about that stuff. They don't understand it; they don't do that. They're wired differently.

At the same time, I don't want you to turn totally paranoid about guys or start feeling uncomfortable or unsafe (if you do feel unsafe, talk to someone about it—you know the saying, "Better safe than sorry"). And I certainly don't want you to decide any guy who has ever had a sexual thought is a total jerk! So please, that isn't my purpose. Don't go overboard.

Here are some major differences.

"There's this one girl who's my friend, and I only want to think of her as a friend, but when she wears skanky clothes, it makes me think about crossing that line. And of course, it's for all the wrong reasons." Mac, 17

"High school is a time to search yourself. See who you are in Jesus. Relationships in high school don't last. Your hormones are so powerful—one day you think this one guy is so cute, but the next week—nah, not so much! I'm choosing not to date in high school." Bethany Dillon

Guys . . .

- are visually stimulated/aroused/turned on
- may see girls as objects to be conquered
- may struggle with pornography
- can get the wrong idea if a girl touches them—even on the arm, back, neck, or leg
- wrestle with controlling their sexual urges

Girls . . .

- are touch/action/romantically stimulated
- can experience feelings of affection when a guy does something kind or thoughtful for them
- get dreamy-eyed over guys (admit it, you've written your first name with a guy's last name, haven't you?)
- feel special when a guy likes them—but they must be aware that his sexual passion might be the driving force behind his charm

Hints

- You'll be helping your guy friends if you don't give them full-body hugs.
- Don't rub a guy's neck or shoulders unless he's related to you.
- You can play with your own hair but not with his.
- Never, under any circumstances, sit in a guy's lap. (Just think of what you're on top of!)
- When it comes to guys and your skin, remember that showing less is best.
- Guys may struggle with their own motives, wanting to be genuinely interested in the whole girl yet being intoxicated with her breasts. Keep them covered.
- Dress modestly. Guys don't need your clothes to stir their thoughts and desires.
- Check your motives! If you *are* purposely showing skin or revealing cleavage to try to get a guy's attention or to get him to ask you out, you're walking a fine line. Beware of tripping into sin.

Keep Your Secret Places Secret!

Since clothes send signals, please make wise wardrobe choices. If a top is sheer, low cut, or skin tight, or it doesn't reach the top edge of your pants, forget it. Cover your abs, hips, and belly button. Keep your secret places secret! If a top looks more like lingerie with its satiny fabric and lace

"Don't be too forward with your feelings—stay mysterious." Jake, 17

"When a girl is showing her cleavage, I have to keep saying to myself, 'Look at her eyes, look at her eyes, look at her eyes.' It's tougher than girls can imagine." Brandon, 16

trim, forget it. It's cut too bare and gives the wrong impression. If a top (or dress or bathing suit) is strapless or halter style, forget it. When it comes to tops, anything that makes you appear braless is *off-limits*. I know you might be wearing a strapless bra, but guys can't always tell. This may sound crude, but if they don't think you have on a bra, they're going to drop their eyes and lock in on your breasts. They'll want to know if those things are bound up or flopping free. No joke. And since we're on the topic of boobies, let's talk nipples. I know you've seen them poking out at school, on the street, at the mall, in the movies, on TV—but that doesn't make it okay. It's not right and not necessary for a guy to see your nipples poking out from your shirt (or dress or swimsuit). He doesn't need to know if you have pea-sized or olive-sized nipples. It's not his business to know if they point straight out, sorta up, or off to the sides. Keep your secret places secret! Purchase a bra that has more than one thin layer of fabric. The ones that are *slightly* padded are best. (I can hear you teeny-busted girls going, "Yes! Thank you, Jesus, for permission to wear a padded bra!") Not only will you be more comfortable, but you won't have to worry about some guy staring at your chest. If you don't agree with me, ask your brother, uncle, or dad! (And watch him turn bright red!)

Low-rise pants are also a challenge. If they're too low, when you bend over or sit down, you'll have a crack attack. And some low-rises are so low in the front that they rest right above a girl's pubic hairline. This, as well as styles like lace-up fronts, is very suggestive to guys. Keep your secret places secret!

So you, B.A.B.E., are faced with a decision.

Are you willing to cover your cleavage and curves?

Are you willing to wear clothes that honor your body as God's temple?

Are you willing to choose not to tempt guys to stare?

Are you willing to be okay with not fitting in by choosing not to wear the same things other girls are wearing?

If you need to spend time praying about it or talking it over with a girlfriend, fine. I'm confident that you'll make the best choice.

> Or don't you know that your body is the temple of the Holy Spirit,
> who lives in you and was given to you by God? You do not belong to
> yourself, for God bought you with a high price. So you must honor
> God with your body.
>
> 1 Corinthians 6:19–20 NLT

Does Sex Make a Guy a Man?

Do you remember the day you started your period? I do. My menstrual cycle decided to make its appearance in the middle of eighth-grade history class. I was horrified. Nevertheless, the menstrual cycle is a definite sign that a girl's body has reached sexual maturity. It doesn't mean her character and emotions are fully developed, but physically speaking, she's passed from girlhood into womanhood.

It's not quite the same for guys. There's nothing specific in our Western culture that really marks when a man becomes a man. We don't have a rite of passage for guys. For instance, in the Jewish culture, a boy has a bar mitzvah at age thirteen. This event marks the end of boyhood and the beginning of his journey into manhood. The way his parents, relatives, teachers, and others relate to him changes. He starts viewing himself in new ways, ways that match his newly acquired responsibilities as a man. The African culture has something similar. Circumcision. My husband and I were leading a team of teens on a mission trip near Narok, Kenya, East Africa. Members of the Maasai tribe invited us to join in on this event and celebration of a young man's entrance into manhood. The boy, surrounded by village men, had to endure the physical pain of having the foreskin on the tip of his penis sliced off (in the American culture, baby boys are circumcised soon after birth). The

Less is best when it comes to showing skin.

men surrounding him hollered, screamed, and moaned, but *he* had to be silent. If he cried or yelled, he would disgrace his family name and he wouldn't be given the gifts a successful boy received—gifts like land, cows, sheep, or goats of his very own. I'm happy to report that he made it through the ordeal without so much as a whimper! From that day on, he was treated like a man and was expected to act like one.

A rite of passage clearly acknowledges a young man's entrance into manhood. Our culture is missing that. Our guys don't have an exact time and place that announces, "Hey, I'm a real man now!"

This is part of what makes sex a bigger deal to some guys. In their opinion, it identifies them as men. But let's follow this logic out. An elephant can have sex. A lizard can have sex. A hamster, a dog, a gorilla, a hippopotamus can all have sex, *but sex will never turn them into men*! They can mate, and they can merge, yet men they will not become. So does having sex really mean a guy has become a man?

Don't you think the real man would be the guy who can control his sexual urges out of obedience to God and out of respect for his future wife? For a guy to do this is extremely hard, but it's not impossible. If a guy tells you he can't control himself as he reaches up your shirt, or if he says it's your fault that he's all hot for you and that now you have to have sex with him, bull crud! Really. I hope you're never in these situations, but if you are, run for your life! Get out of there. It's times like these when a guy may strong-arm a girl, forcing her to have sex. It's called date rape. It's not an act of passion; it's a crime of violence. Be wise. Think ahead; plan ahead. Don't get yourself in a compromising situation. (This is a great reason not to single date in your teen years—guys have a harder time controlling things, because they're still emotionally immature.)

Speaking Up

Whether girls like it or not, most of the time we're the ones who must say no to sex. Not only when you're twirling your purity ring and not dating anyone. That's when it's easy. But when a babe-a-licious hunk of guy is moving in to kiss your neck—that's when it *really* counts! And that's when you need to say no. Don't wait until something else happens.

I've talked to girls who have been afraid to say no. They just sort of freeze up, letting the guy do what he wants. Later they're upset and hurt, feeling violated and used.

This is when a girl's self-image heads for the toilet. She never wanted to let a guy touch her or use her like that. She wanted to be a total virgin. She's mad at herself for not being brave.

She sees herself as dirty and trashed. And if the guy tells his buddies, her reputation gets ruined.

Please understand that no male *ever* has the right to touch your body, especially when you're saying no (I pray you're saying no). This is true for the guy who pulls you into a prolonged bear hug as well as the one who tries more. You aren't obligated to him. Even if it is prom night or winter formal!

Have a plan. First, grab the wrist of whichever hand is going where it shouldn't. Second, open your mouth and say "no" or "stop." Make it short. Don't launch into a five minute explanation about why you think you shouldn't go any further. It will be too late, and he probably won't be listening anyway. Third, move! Back away, sit up, push him away, or whatever so that your body matches your words. Make it say no! So take action and speak up at the same time. Then start talking your head off, say you have to go to the bathroom, whatever you need to do to—just get out.

If you need help, get it. Never be embarrassed to call your parents or a friend to come pick you up. Never be afraid to call 911 if you're being threatened. The main thing is that you need to protect yourself if the situation calls for it. Naturally, my hope is that you won't need any drastic tactics because you'll choose to steer clear of single dating and alone time with guys during their testosterone-intense years. Think about it. They're less mature than you (yep, there's documented proof), their emotions are less developed than yours, they think self-control has something to do with a remote or an Xbox, and their hormones are firing like a semiautomatic rifle—fast and furious! Their bodies are on fire, and you're a bucket of ice-cold water! Their flames cause them to say stuff they don't mean, like, "I really, really like you. I love you. I can see myself with you forever. No one's as hot as you. You're beautiful. I've never felt this way about anyone before . . ."

If he's over twenty-five, has finished his education, has a steady job giving him enough gas money for his very own car, has put an engagement ring on your finger, has set a wedding date, and has put a down payment on a house—okay, then you can believe him! But he still needs to wait until the honeymoon for your beautiful body to become his.

Flip Side

Your turn. Because I've seen the way some girls flaunt themselves at guys, I have to say this. If the tables are turned, and *you* are the one pushing *him* to kiss you, to touch you, to lie down with you, or to get naked and have sex with you, stop it! Stop it! Sex won't guarantee he'll be your boyfriend. Sex won't prove you love him or he loves you. Sex won't promise a commitment to the future. Sex won't superglue you together as a couple. Instead, it will break your heart. It will leave

"Now that I'm seriously walking with God, I look back and feel really badly about all the girls I lied to just to get sex, or at least get them to let me under their clothes. I feel like a jerk. There's one girl I can't stop thinking about—I know I hurt her very badly." a guy, blond, blue eyes, age 19

you emotionally devastated. It takes away your virginity, your self-esteem, your self-respect. It steals unexplainable things that will be gone forever.

Back up and back off.

God says no to premarital sex. God says no to fornication (anything that leads up to sex). God says no because he loves you and wants to protect you from the physical, emotional, psychological, and spiritual damage that can result from this sin. Sin? Yep, let's just call it what it is, call it what the Bible calls it. These verses tell it like it is.

> But sexual sin is never right: our bodies were not made for that, but for the Lord, and the Lord wants to fill our bodies with himself. . . . Run from sex sin. No other sin affects the body as this one does. . . . So use every part of your body to give glory back to God, because he owns it.
>
> 1 Corinthians 6:13, 18, 20 TLB

> For God wants you to be holy and pure, and to keep clear of all sexual sin so that each of you will marry in holiness. . . . For God has not called us to be dirty-minded and full of lust, but to be holy and clean. If anyone refuses to live by these rules he [she] is not disobeying the rules of men but of God.
>
> 1 Thessalonians 4:3–4, 7–8 TLB

If you're purposely trying to sexually tease or tempt a guy, you're sinning and may cause him to sin.

> Determine this—not to put an obstacle or a stumbling block in a brother's way.
>
> Romans 14:13 NASB

This is God's teaching! This is what he says! If we trip someone else up because of our actions, our lustful desires, our little games, then not only do we sin, but we cause the other person to fall into sin too. We become doubly responsible. What's the key to keeping yourself from doing such things?

Love. Not for the guy, but for God.

Bottom line, do you love the Lord enough that you'll choose to do what he wants you to do, to obey him? Jesus said,

If you love me, obey me.

John 14:15 TLB

If you love Me, you will keep My commandments.

John 14:15 NASB

Ouch. Did you feel a sting in your heart, a kick in your gut? This is tough stuff. This is "where the rubber meets the road" stuff. This is "will you cross the line or not" stuff. This is radical obedience stuff. It isn't casual Christianity.

Obedience proves love.

B.A.B.E., when we find ourselves doing the right thing only when it's convenient or will work in our favor, forget it. That's being fake. There's no love in that. Or if we purposely choose to disobey God, the light of love is blown out. It's hard to be faced with the truth that you might not love God as much as you thought you did. Girlfriend, the only way to grow in your love for God is through knowing him better, more intimately.

It goes like this: To obey him, you must love him. To love him, you must know him. To know him, you must study the book that

Sexual chemistry is one of God's best gifts to humanity, but it's intended to help define attraction *before* marriage and define the intimacy of that relationship only *after* marriage.

reveals who he is: the Bible. Yes, it takes time and effort, but it will be invested into the very core of who you are—a child of God.

Until you're married, the skinny on sex is *no* sex. That would be called abstinence—it means to abstain, to intentionally choose *not* to do something. In this case, not to have sex. Okay, then, if we choose to commit to God's way and prove our love through obedience, what do we do when we find ourselves wanting or craving that kind of relationship with a guy? Great question. Let's explore it.

What's Up with My Body? Handling Sexual Feelings

"I don't know what to do about the way I feel," Trish explained in her email. "There are moments when my body seems to be yearning for something, like it wants to be touched in ways I don't even understand yet. I'm a virgin, and I want to stay a virgin, but what's happening? I mean, I don't even have a boyfriend, but this is happening. My best friend and her guy are weakening. She told me how her body seems to take over once her boyfriend starts messing with her breasts. She's worried, and I'm worried for her. What are we supposed to do?"

Trish's body is awake to feelings of sexual excitement. She is *sex-cited*! Girls have sexual urges just like guys do. They tend to be less intense and less frequent, but they happen. The female body has been designed for sex—within the marriage relationship—and to find it pleasurable. As the body becomes aroused (sexually awake), changes start taking place. Tingling skin becomes more sensitive, blood flow to the vagina increases, nipples harden, pulse increases—this is how God designed the female body to respond. Yet he also gives us important instructions. Listen up:

Promise me . . . not to awaken love until the time is right.

Song of Solomon 2:7 NLT

Until the time is right! You already know God wants a person to experience all of this only when she's married. First is the spiritual union that occurs during the marriage ceremony. Following that is physical union—sex! Getting it in the right order will save a girl so much grief.

But if waiting for "I do" is driving you crazy, here are ten ideas suggested by my single friends, age twenty to seventy-one!

1. Pray. Ask the Lord to fill you with self-control and to calm your body. Ask him to grant you the gift of celibacy until your wedding night. Celibacy means to remain single and sexually abstinent for the purpose of serving God (1 Corinthians 7:8–9).

2. Change your focus. Get your mind on something else and keep it there.

3. Definitely go do something physical to release the built-up tension—jog, bike, roller blade—just choose something aerobic that will physically exhaust you.

4. Take a cold shower—it works for guys!

5. Don't allow yourself to look at porn or let your remote land on MTV, VH1, or other stations that carry sexually explicit content. That will increase your desire, not remove it. It can also make you feel guilty or cause lust.

6. Call a friend and get lost in girl talk.

7. Choose only group dates, not single dates. Single dating sets you up in a romantic situation that will fuel the very feelings you're trying to avoid. It may sound radical, but it works!

8. Read the Bible. The Holy Spirit will help give you peace as you concentrate on what you're reading. God is faithful.

9. The jury seems to be out on whether or not it's okay for you to rub the areas that feel sexcited. Try to avoid it, since it can quickly (and innocently) become a habit. Keep in mind that the feelings themselves aren't wrong, but what you do with them might be.

10. Avoid romance novels and movies with steamy scenes.

How can a young man [woman] keep his [her] way pure?
By living according to your word.
I seek you with all my heart;
do not let me stray from your commands.

Psalm 119:9–10 NIV

Is It Ever Too Late?

This question has a two-letter answer. No! See, we have a God who sent his very own Son to earth to die on the cross in our place, to take the punishment we deserve for messing up. Our heavenly Father loves you and me that much. He offers forgiveness. He offers a fresh start. He promises to make us white as snow.

If you've been sexually involved with a guy, seek God's forgiveness and forgive yourself. Then start over. Just like he told the woman caught in adultery, Jesus would say to you, "I don't condemn you. Go on your way, but don't sin anymore" (John 8:11, my paraphrase). My precious friend, do whatever it takes to save yourself from this moment forward.

With all of this sex talk, the obvious question is, Can guys and girls *really* just be friends? Is it possible for a nice guy to casually talk to a girl without her thinking he's head over heels or wants to date her? Can a girl want to get to know a guy because she finds him interesting without his thoughts drifting off to something R-rated?

Yes! It happens when you focus on building friendships, not romantic relationships, with guys. There's more on this coming up! First, let's see how guys and girls can be spiritually different. ●

GOD IS GREAT, GOD IS GOOD

Understanding Spiritual Differences

My dad taught me this bedtime prayer. I knew it was goofy, of course, but this is the version that was embedded into my heart and mind.

> Now I lay me down to sleep
> With ten apples at my feet.
> If I should die before I wake,
> You'll know I died with a bellyache!

Ten apples in one night would give anyone a bellyache! This is the only version of this prayer I'd ever heard. So picture me as an adult, sitting in a Sunday school class at a church where my husband was the new pastor. The teacher makes reference to this simple, sweet childhood prayer. Then he begins to recite it.

Now I lay me down to sleep.
[I'm thinking, yep, I know this part.]
I pray the Lord my soul to keep.
[Hey, wait, that doesn't sound right—it's nice, but something's odd.]
If I should die before I wake,
[Okay, now we're back on track.]
I pray the Lord my soul to take.
[My soul to take? Where's the part about the apples and the bellyache?]

"We all learned this prayer as children." His voice began to fade as it struck me that my dad had never taught me this "other" version. Apparently, this was the *real* version, the spiritual version. *That ornery father of mine! He had me praying about my belly instead of my soul!* The thought just about caused me to spit out the sip of hot coffee that had just entered my mouth. I was so ticked that I instantly began to tear up. And you know how it is, girls, when something hits you just right—you sorta lose it. I lost it. My face contorted as the tears flowed. I grabbed my Bible, got up, and headed for the kitchen (our class was meeting in the fellowship hall, where the cooking facilities were located). With my hand over my lips, I tried to muffle the crazy hyenalike sounds coming from my throat!

I'm sure the class wondered what was wrong with me. Perhaps they thought I was so moved by the lesson on prayer that it brought me to tears. I'm sure they wondered what the heck I was doing in the kitchen for the final twenty minutes of class! But I couldn't go back out there. Every time I thought about my dad, the laughter and tears started all over again. My dad, the guy who got suspended from parochial school because he cut class to go the theater to see *Gone with the Wind*! I should have known. Yet in his defense, I have to say that in the tough times, I've seen my dad's faith in God shining through.

Girls and guys are spiritually different.

These are general observations, not documented facts, but they seem to ring true.

Guys . . .

- tend to be less expressive about their spiritual lives
- are more private about what God is doing in their lives
- often have a faith that runs deeper than it appears on the surface
- tend to approach God using logic, wanting reasons and proof
- tend to be independent and self-assured, so they can forget to ask God for help
- may turn to God as a last resort (they try to figure it out by themselves first)
- tend to be leaders in the church (they want it to run well and efficiently)
- are quicker than most girls in the forgiveness department

Girls . . .

- tend to be more expressive about their relationship with the Lord
- are more apt to ask questions and not be embarrassed if they don't understand something
- tend to seek God's guidance before attempting to figure something out alone
- tend to be service oriented in the church (they care that needs are being met)
- are good prayer partners (unless they use what they learn about others to spread gossip)
- can seem more devoted to the Lord
- spend more time in group Bible study

Hints

- Never laugh at the way a guy worships.
- Don't tease him about what he says during a prayer.

- Don't imitate him if he messes up reading a Bible verse out loud.
- Don't judge him. He'll see it as rejection, and that will shut him down and close his spirit toward you. A good friend is a safe place.
- Know that God has called him to be a leader, protector, provider, and spiritual head of his future household. Encourage these qualities in him. ●

GOD DID IT ON *PURPOSE*!

The Burning Question . . .
WHY?

The facts are in. Guys are so incredibly different from girls—major opposites. The burning question you might be asking is, Why? With all this information, what do we conclude? Guys are unique, weird, strange, alienlike creatures that need to be locked up in Boyland? There are days you'll think that sounds like a great plan. But that's not God's plan. He purposely created Adam. He purposely had Adam name all the animals so he would see that they were way too different from him—and see that the best B.A.B.E. for him was not among this group. Because of this, when God caused Adam to fall into a deep sleep, removed one of his ribs, and then used it to create a woman, Adam knew instantly in his heart that this, the beautiful creature God brought to him, was the perfect fit. Yet after a while, he realized that she didn't look like him, didn't act like him, didn't think like him, didn't do much of *anything* like him—but oh, how he loved her.

Yes, they were opposites. Yet opposite is God's plan! Why would God choose that? So there could be friction? No. So there would be conflict? No. So they could **complement** each other? Yes!

I love to paint landscapes and capture God's colorful creation on canvas. One day I was painting a garden scene. I started with bright yellow snapdragons, then placed orange marigolds to the left of them. On the right, I painted vibrant purple pansies. Wow! I discovered that the orange next to the yellow snapdragons was pleasant, almost calming, but the purple popped! It drew my attention. It seemed to create a visual energy. Why? Because yellow and purple are direct *opposites* on the color wheel. In the art world, these are known as complementary colors. Opposites have an incredible ability to bring out the best in each other; side by side they create an energetic pop! They complement each other.

Notice that I didn't say opposites **complete** each other. Adam didn't complete Eve or vice versa. We're not half a person until we find someone to suddenly make us whole! This is a gigantic misconception that tons of teens (and adults) buy into. If it were true, then God did a grave injustice in allowing Jesus to be incomplete throughout his entire life since he didn't date and never married. How odd would that be? How unfair? And why would God want us to be like Jesus if Jesus was only half a guy? Think about it.

Guys don't complete girls. Girls don't complete guys.

Yet that's the impression you'll pick up in our society. Don't be brainwashed. Be wise and always check stuff out by what the Bible teaches. In this case, when it comes to the idea of men and women, males and females completing each other, I just don't see it.

The Bible plainly states that we who have placed our trust in Jesus have been made complete in him (Colossians 2:10).

As a B.A.B.E. who has, hopefully, come to understand that you're beautiful in God's eyes, that you're accepted by God, that you're blessed by God with special abilities and spiritual gifts, and that you're eternally significant, your very existence has been *on* purpose and *for* a purpose. Based on these biblical truths, how in the world would God have left you incomplete and dependent on another human being to make you whole?

My valuable, talented, loving, gifted, babe-a-licious friend, you aren't in need of anything in terms of a guy completing you.

- A guy isn't the answer to your loneliness or sadness; these are heart issues that can be truly fulfilled only by the Lord himself.

He knows where you hurt, and he knows how to heal you. If you need extra insight, go to a female counselor who loves the Lord.

- A guy won't be the answer to your financial woes; God has said a ton about how to make and manage your money in the Bible. He knew you would need his guidance, and he's got you covered on this one in his Word. (Look at the teen books and surveys available by going to www.crown.org. Click on "Your Family" and scroll down to "Teens." Study and know this stuff—it's an investment in yourself and your financial future.)

- A guy isn't the answer to your boring days or unexciting future; God alone knows what's up for you. He has a plan for your life—but if you don't seek him and spend time in the Bible, in prayer, and in praise, it's possible for you to miss that plan.

- A guy isn't the answer to you feeling better about yourself and feeling more socially acceptable. God has given you the ultimate acceptance—his! The A in B.A.B.E. is for accepted. If you truly grab hold of this concept and let it get inside your soul, and if you've made God your audience, then you'll feel positive about yourself regardless of your social status or love life.

- A guy isn't the answer to your longing to be loved; God loves you beyond words. The depth of his love is evidenced in the giving of his only Son as payment for all of your sin debts, resulting in your eternal salvation (John 3:16). The sincerity of his love can be felt in his promise to never leave you, fail you, or forsake you (Hebrews 13:5). God's love doesn't come and go—it's everlasting (Jeremiah 31:3). Married women who go through times of feeling unloved by their husbands and singles who jump from one relationship to another will tell you that the fulfillment of your deepest longing to be loved doesn't come from a member of the male species! It comes from a personal, intimate love relationship with God through Jesus. Period.

God, in his infinite wisdom, created the sexes to be opposite so they would *complement* one another. Therefore, they have the ability to bring out the best in each other, to make each other shine! ●

God calls some people to stay single for the purpose of being available and ministry focused. It's a high calling. Certainly he wouldn't do this if in any way singleness was an indication of one being incomplete.

Love Affair

She first heard the rumor at school. A group of students from the FCA (Fellowship of Christian Athletes) group were huddled together speaking just slightly above a whisper. But still, she heard it.

He liked her for more than a friend.

He wanted to get to know her and for her to know him. *He certainly isn't pushy,* she thought. *He must be waiting for me to come to him, to make the first move.*

A faint recollection of a childhood song passed through her consciousness . . . "Jesus loves me this I know, for the Bible tells me so." *Wait, maybe he's already made the first move.*

Could it be? Close to being convinced, she gave it the final test, the daisy test. *He loves me. He loves me not. He loves me. He loves me not. He loves me.* Joy began to bubble up deep inside her as she closed her eyes, lifted her chin, and let the warmth of the sun envelop her. Then came peace. It lifted the burdens of her heart. To her it was an "okay" that she should do it. She should respond to his invitation to know him, to surrender to him, to become his child.

Oh, Jesus, it's me. I've known your love, but I was afraid you wouldn't accept me as I am. Now I know you will. I got your invitation, and my RSVP is YES! Come into my heart, invade my life, teach me to love you more every day.

In the beginning, she chose to keep it under wraps—not quite ready to be found out. But the tender love letters he wrote her were hard to keep to herself. And his attentiveness to her—always available and eager to meet with her—was something she wanted to brag about.

So she leaked the news. She was having an affair—a love affair. And she wanted the whole world to know that his name was Jesus.

EXPERT INSIGHT

Pam Farrel Talks about Boys and Boxes, Girls and Pasta!

Andrea: I've been talking to the girls about the fact that God made girls and guys different in almost *every* way. Why do you think he did that?

Pam: The Bible tells us that people are made in God's image, and I think God, in his wisdom, gave guys some great traits and girls some other great traits.

Andrea: I love the title of your book, *Men Are Like Waffles, Women Are Like Spaghetti*. Talk to us about the waffle idea first. What does that mean?

Pam: Guys process life in boxes. If you look down at a waffle, you see a collection of boxes separated by walls. The boxes are all separate from each other. That's typically how a male processes life. A guy's thinking is divided up into boxes that have room for one issue and one issue only. The first issue of life goes in the first box, the second goes in the second box, and so on. The typical male then spends time in one box at a time and one box only. When he's in the garage tinkering around, he's in the garage tinkering. When he's watching TV, he's simply watching TV. That's why he looks

Pam Farrel is the award-winning author of *Men Are Like Waffles, Women Are Like Spaghetti*. You can check out her website at www.masterfulliving.com.

like he's in a trance and can ignore everything else going on around him. Social scientists call this "compartmentalizing"—putting life and responsibilities into different compartments or boxes.

Andrea: Okay, so boys are like boxes and girls are like pasta?

Pam: In contrast to guys' waffle-like approach, girls process life more like a plate of spaghetti. If you look at a plate of spaghetti, you notice that there are individual noodles that all touch one another. If you attempted to follow one noodle around the plate, you would intersect a lot of other noodles, and you might even switch seamlessly to another noodle. That's how women face life. Every thought and issue is connected to every other thought and issue in some way. Scientists call this "integration." This is why girls are typically better at *multitasking* than guys are. Girls can talk on the phone, paint their toenails, make a shopping list, plan a student council meeting, and do Pilates without skipping a beat.

Andrea: I was chatting with some girls after youth group about the fact that guys get lost in our conversations with them.

Pam: Right! Spaghetti can weave all over the plate. We can intertwine topics. But guys can't jump from box to box that fast. They just don't follow us like our girlfriends do.

Andrea: Does that have anything to do with the fact that girls tend to talk fast and talk so much more than most guys?

Pam: Definitely! It's hard for us to relate to, but the fact is that most males have boxes in their waffles that have no words. There are thoughts in these boxes, but the thoughts don't turn into words. Not all the wordless boxes have thoughts, however. There are actually boxes in the average man's waffle that contain no words and no thoughts. These boxes are just as blank as a white sheet of paper. They're *empty*! To help relieve stress in his life, a guy will "park" in these boxes to relax. Amazingly, girls seem to notice this, so they invariably ask, "What are you thinking about?" He immediately panics, like a deer caught in the headlights. His eyes start darting back and forth hoping to find some box in close proximity that has words in it. He can look like he's trying to hide something, but the truth is, he's trying to find something: words!

Andrea: Based on the nature of girls, what are some incorrect conclusions they might draw about guys?

Pam: When guys answer with short responses, girls can think they're rude or disinterested. News flash! Most guys answer *everything* with short answers! Guys aren't shallow—they're just different. Some girls may think guys are unfriendly because they rarely talk about their feelings. Guys share feelings very slowly, but they do have them! Their feelings are in the bottom of each waffle box, and a girl has to be a patient listener to get to them.

Andrea: So if they're not big talkers and not as emotional as girls, how might a girl be able to know what a guy is all about?

Pam: Pay attention to what he shares with you. Say a guy has a nice car. He may say, "Want to go for a ride?" It isn't all about him showing off his car. He's saying, "I want to be with you. I like your company." Some guys offer to fix stuff for you; others

A Good Guy Is a F.I.N.E. Guy
First place in his heart is God.
Integrity and character define him.
Nice is his middle name—
    don't take any abuse, B.A.B.E.!
Encourages you to be all God
    designed you to be.

Pam Farrel

offer to help you with a class or a project. (Maybe they're good at math and you aren't, so they might offer to study with you.) Or they may offer to carry things for you. Their inner character will show, but you have to look closely, or you'll miss it.

Andrea: Amen! ●

"If guys are like waffles,
then waffles rock."
Lindsey, 15

WHY IS HE LIKE THAT?

The Truth
about BO

If you thought I was going to launch into a discussion about the horrifying ways guys can smell, sorry! That would be another whole book! When I say BO, I'm not referring to body odor. I'm referring to *birth order*! That's right, birth order.

When was he born? No, not the time of day, the season, or the year. This isn't about him being a Capricorn or a Leo (that stuff is bogus anyway). This is about when he was born within his family. Did he appear on planet Earth as the first child in the fam, the last child, or somewhere in the middle? Or is he an only child?

Knowing what order a guy was born into his family can reveal a lot of helpful information about him. So in your quest to understand the guys in your house, your class, your youth group, your space, find out their birth order.

Who would think that affects anything? Tons of psychologists, that's who. Those who study human behavior have noted that the order of people's birth presents a unique set of dynamics that influences them big time. Their placement in the lineup among their siblings does matter.

Understanding BO and educating yourself on this will give you more insight into the inhabitants of Boyland. It will enable you to maneuver your way through this foreign land with greater success! How? Well, remember, we're on a journey to understand guys. We want to know *why* they think what they think, say what they say, and do what they do! This will assist you in having some awesome friendships and, later on, a tighter marriage with the guy God has already chosen for you. Cool, huh? Okay, think of your brother (if you have one) or a guy friend. Then ask yourself the following:

1. Is he sorta charming in a boyish way? Does he like to be the center of attention? Does he show off? Is he well liked, and does he have lots of friends as well as different types of friends? Would he rather be with a crowd than home alone playing computer games? Does he sometimes blame others when life doesn't go his way? Does he have a hard time making commitments and/or following through? Is he a hang-loose guy?

2. Is he way too serious sometimes? Is he always busy—taking on new projects or doing too much? Does he like to be an officer in clubs, or has he

run for class office? Is he dependable? Is he picky or controlling about the way things get done? Is he super organized about everything from his homework to his car to his personal stuff? Does he sweat the small stuff because he's into details and hates to fail? Is he a high achiever?

3. Is he an independent thinker—not really a go-with-the-crowd type? Is he way too agreeable at times because he wants to avoid conflict? Is he a people pleaser? Is he a super loyal friend? Is he gifted at helping two people who are mad at each other work it out? Does he ever feel left out of his family? Is he a deep thinker?

4. Is he uptight a lot of the time? Is he focused on how life affects him more than how it affects others? Is he picky to the extreme? Does he want to be in charge? Has he always behaved like an adult—even when he

was younger? Does he use words most teen guys don't know? Does he hang with guys older than himself? Does he enjoy being alone? Does he see himself as the center of the universe?

Which of the above description best fits the guy you had in mind? 1, 2, 3, or 4?

Before I tell you which BO matches these descriptions, I want you to take a guess. Think through the position of each BO and what special circumstances might come with that position. For example, the oldest child often has to care for younger kids in his family, making him rank high on the responsibility scale, while the youngest in the family is used to having others watch out for him, so he ends up the carefree, fun guy! Now think through your own birth order, your siblings' birth orders, and which of the above descriptions fit them.

Ready to take a gamble?

The first description is of the _____ child. The second description fits the _____ child. The third has to be the _____ child, and the last description must be the _____ child.

Let's see how you did. One is the lastborn, the baby of the family. Two is the oldest. Three is the middle child—could be number two or three in the family, just not the firstborn or the lastborn. Four matches up with the only kid in the family (who could have a mix of oldest child and youngest child characteristics, since he's both). Remember, these aren't set-in-stone descriptions, meaning that no unique God-designed guy can be totally pegged, but these are well-studied observations. This birth order info gives you another piece of the "I'm trying to figure him out" puzzle, thus allowing you to know more of who guys are and what they're all about.

Now, allow me to toss the salad and see if you can still follow me. Reality is, half of all

What's *your* birth order? Do you see yourself in these descriptions? What are you learning about *you*?

American families are a remix. This presents all sorts of new, difficult, and complicated situations, including birth order. See, if a guy is firstborn in his original family, he develops those firstborn characteristics. But then, if a remarriage brings in an older stepsister, he's no longer top dog. Or if a baby in the family (whose older siblings are off to college) is blended with two new younger sisters (the oldest of whom just became a middle child), he is now the oldest in the home, the firstborn position. He may be accused of acting immature and irresponsible most of the time. That's because he's going to have to learn and grow into his new position, which comes with responsibility and leadership. Life gets complicated, huh?

Okay, moving on. Here's how this BO info helps.

When your male lab partner seems uptight about the experiment going just right and is picky, picky, picky, you can predict that he's a firstborn and not take his obsession with perfection as a personal jab at you (like he thinks you're going to blow the thing up).

When a lastborn Boyland inhabitant appears to be working his teasing game on every breathing thing wearing a bra (and appears more flirtatious than overly friendly), you can laugh him off! More than trying to pick up all the girls, he's just being his fun-loving, show-off self.

When your oldest brother yells at you for not doing something the way he would do it, you can chalk his control freakishness up to what? Being the first kid in the family and wanting to please the parents.

When a guy seems to slide from one peer group to another, you can bet he's a middle child searching for his place to fit in rather than a weirdo guy who just can't make friends.

Are you getting this? Catching on? Do you see that some guy isn't just purposely trying to drive you nuts? Great!

Take this B.A.B.E. challenge: Be intentional (do it for a reason) about your well-established habit of guy watching. (Hey, its okay. We all do it when we're single and unattached—it's a bona fide girl hobby.) Observe their actions and attitudes. Study how they handle situations. Listen to how they phrase sentences and express themselves (or don't express themselves). This will help you be quick to spot birth order. It will help you relax and smile, knowing that the guy is just being who he is. And that's totally okay with God, so it can be totally okay with you. After all, God is the One who determined his order of birth. ●

THE BIBLE GUY MATCHUP

Before we take a final exit from this babe-a-licious birth order info, we really need to take a fast look at some Bible dudes. Skim over these facts, keeping our birth order teaching in mind. Be prepared to do a matchup.

John—He responded immediately to the invitation to follow Jesus. He was attentive to Jesus and his needs, referring to himself as "the disciple whom Jesus loved" (John 21:20 NIV). He was in Jesus's inner circle of friends. He asked for special placement in the kingdom of God and was seen as selfish by the other disciples. God used him to write five books of the New Testament (John, 1 John, 2 John, 3 John, and Revelation).

James—He stayed behind to help his father with the fishing business when Jesus first called him, but at Jesus's second invitation, James willingly joined in. He was one of Jesus's three closest friends and the first to be killed for his faith in Christ. He and his brother John were known as "Sons of Thunder" due to their outbursts of anger (Mark 3:17 NIV).

Joseph—He was known by his brothers as the happy, confident dreamer who was favored and spoiled by their father. His brothers captured him, sold him as a slave, and told their father he was dead. Through God's plan and Joseph's unwavering obedience, Joseph was promoted from a slave to the ruler of Egypt who saved his family (God's people) from famine.

Reuben—He was Joseph's brother, the only one who stood up for him. He convinced his other brothers to throw Joseph into a deep pit to die naturally instead of murdering him. Reuben secretly planned to come back to rescue Joseph, but when he returned to the pit, Joseph was gone—the brothers had sold him as a slave.

Luke—He was a well-educated medical doctor and an exact historian who recorded Jesus's life with detail and accuracy in the Gospel of Luke. The book of Acts, which documented the days of the early church after Jesus returned to heaven, was also penned by Dr. Luke. He was known for his compassion and his faithfulness to travel with the apostle Paul.

Aaron—He was assigned by God to be his brother Moses's spokesperson. The times he was left in charge, he would manage to make a mess of things because he gave in to the pressure from the people (yep, he allowed them to worship a golden calf instead of God). Plus, he got in trouble with God for complaining and criticizing Moses. He was the first high priest in Israel.

Just like a leopard doesn't change its spots, a guy typically doesn't change his! Learn to appreciate his divine design—inside and out!

John the Baptist—He was a loner whom God used to prepare people for Jesus's arrival. He baptized those who repented and wanted a clean heart before God. He lived in the woods, wore camel-skin clothes, and had a yummy diet of honey and locusts. He was beheaded for speaking out against the sinful lifestyle of King Herod.

Match 'em up by drawing a line from the dude to his birth order:

John	only dude
James	middle dude
Joseph	baby dude
Reuben	middle dude
Luke	oldest dude
Aaron	oldest dude
John the Baptist	middle dude

Answer key:
John the Baptist—only dude; Aaron—middle dude; Luke—middle dude; Reuben—oldest dude; Joseph—baby dude; James—oldest dude; John—middle dude.

Innies and Outies

There are many things that make guys different from girls, right? And there are many things that make guys different from each other, right? Well, here's another one! Are you ready for this? It's a great tool for figuring out why one guy reacts one way and another guy reacts the completely opposite way. And every guy is either one or the other. Innies and outies. That's what I'm saying! Take a typical group of Boylanders, do a quick interview, and each one of them will be one or the other. Some guys are innies—they're somewhat withdrawn—while other guys are totally out-there outies. I'm *not* talking belly buttons—you know that, right? I'm referring to how a guy relates to and interacts with others. This is part of the way God designed him.

If he tends to be a shy guy, he's an innie—an **introvert**!

If he tends to be a sassy stud muffin, he's an outie—he's got **extrovert** written all over him!

An introvert . . .

- is quiet and timid
- is a good listener
- values close friends
- thinks deeply about the meaning of life and situations
- is totally comfortable being alone
- is aware of his inner world, his thoughts and feelings
- can be hard to get to know—he's more private
- can seem unfriendly
- is the strong, silent type

Hey, B.A.B.E., are you a pleasant introvert or a bubbly extrovert?

An extrovert . . .

- is talkative and outgoing
- dislikes silence, so he fills it with words or music
- is friendly and people oriented
- is most comfortable with other people around
- can be an attention hog
- is aware of his outer world, what's going on outside himself
- can seem annoying
- can be easy to get to know on the surface
- is usually uninhibited and unconcerned about what others think of him

My two favorite teen guys in the world are each a cookie-cutter copy of these descriptions. Cody, my auburn-haired, brown-eyed nephew from my side of the family, is 99.9 percent extrovert. His friendly, outgoing, and talkative self was set in stone by kindergarten—the teacher couldn't keep the kid in his seat! He was busy checking out his classmates' craft projects or trying to get someone to join him in a game of Ninja Turtle Takedown. When I'd get the chance to visit him during his growing-up years, Cody always wanted to *do* something—play hide-and-seek, wrestle, build forts, kick the soccer ball around the backyard, and harass his two younger sisters (oh, wait, he still likes that one). And whatever it was, the louder the better! Being an introvert myself, he always wore me out!

As a teen, Cody is still very social and would rather be hanging with friends or playing lacrosse (a group sport) than quietly reading or conquering a computer game. He excels in football and wrestling and bass guitar (yeah, he wants to be on stage in a band), and he actually *likes* to talk on the phone or IM.

Cullen is just the opposite. Quiet, quiet, quiet! Cullen is my blond-haired, hazel-eyed nephew from my husband's side of the family. Growing up, he was shy, liked to work alone quietly, and was a great student because he paid attention to the teacher instead of everyone else around him! When I'd visit, I could barely get him to talk to me. He was far more content when I read him books, played a board game, or watched a Veggie Tales video with him.

As a teen, Cullen is still on the shy side, and I have to make a concentrated effort to ask him lots of questions (yeah, he hates that, but how else can I get to know him, right?). All the info he gained as a young reader has landed him in the gifted classes and at the top of his class. He excels in science and band (he blows a mean trumpet) and is on the football team. In his hang time, you can find him fishing or on the computer.

Soon these two dudes I adore (that's my job as an aunt) are going to meet for the first time. One lives in Virginia, one in Florida. We're all headed to Hilton Head Island, South Carolina, for a week of fun in the sun. It will be a kick for me to watch this duo interact. Truly, they might just become fast friends. See, if they were both introverts, they might sit around in total silence! That could get boring. If they were both extroverts, they would be competing for the center of attention and constantly trying to one-up each other. If they were exactly alike, they might come away saying, "You know, I didn't really like that guy so much." What a sad aunt I would be! But since they're opposites, they might be a great balance.

When it comes to a guy being an innie or an outie, there's no right or wrong. It's just part of who he is. Knowing that some guys aren't really boring or stuck up just because they're not big talkers will help you understand them much better. They're introverts. On the other hand, when a guy is overly friendly and talkative and jokes around with you, that doesn't mean he wants to ask you out! He might just be an outie being the fun-loving guy he is! Appreciate them just the way they are!

A final thought: every guy (just like you and me) can be a mix of introvert and extrovert depending on the situation he's in. An introvert might really put himself out there at football camp or history day competition. An extrovert might pull way back in a room of strangers.

Oh, and FYI: even if a guy is an extrovert, he probably won't gush about his emotions or what's going on in his life. Remember, he's still a typical guy! ●

Seeing Him as God Does

As a B.A.B.E., you've come to understand that you're **beautiful** in God's eyes. You've been handcrafted by him, and he adores your one-of-a-kind look. You're **accepted** by him and have made him your audience of One. You don't have to impress anyone or change to fit in. You belong to God, and he loves you as you are. You've also discovered that God has **blessed** you with special abilities that may be musical, athletic, academic, domestic, etc. Plus, you know you've been blessed with spiritual gifts like leadership, encouragement, service, or teaching (see "Extra Stuff" at the back of this book for more on spiritual gifts). Finally, you've felt your value and worth in the kingdom of God as you use your gifts for **eternally significant** purposes (which, of course, makes *you* eternally significant!).

This may come as a shocking new thought, but God sees guys just like he sees you. Appealing to his eye, acceptable through Christ, with gifts and abilities galore, and with specific assignments with their names on them. It's our heavenly Father's ultimate goal for each of his guys to grow closer and closer to the image of Jesus.

When God steps back and gives his Boylanders the once over, he says . . .

You are my child, adopted into my family as my very own (see John 1:12; Ephesians 1:5). *You're a full-fledged member, entitled to an inheritance.*

You are born of me, and the evil one cannot touch you (see 1 John 5:18). *You are my property!*

You are a member of Christ's body (see 1 Corinthians 12:27). *You are his hands and feet, his eyes and ears, here to serve.*

You are a partaker of my divine nature (see 2 Peter 1:3–4). *You have everything you need to live a godly life.*

You are created in my likeness (see Genesis 1:26–27). *You have my qualities growing in you as you are faithful to seek me.*

You are fearfully and wonderfully made (see Psalm 139:13–14). *You are not just carelessly tossed together.*

You are chosen by my Son, Jesus, and called his friend (see John 15:15–16). *You are not a slave, not a neighbor, not an acquaintance, but a friend!*

You are the home of my Holy Spirit, who lives in you (see John 14:16–18; 1 Corinthians 6:19). *You are more than flesh and bones; you are a hangout for the Holy Spirit.*

You are forgiven (see 1 John 1:9). *Even when you blow it big time, even when you do it over and over.*

You are holy and blameless in my sight (see Ephesians 1:4). *Because of Jesus's death and resurrection, I see you as faultless!*

You have been bought with a price and belong to me (see 1 Corinthians 6:20). *You are paid in full with the crucifixion of Jesus.*

You are redeemed (see Ephesians 1:14). *You have been given new and everlasting value.*

You are loved (see John 3:16; Ephesians 2:4). *Even when it feels like no one else loves you, I always do.*

You cannot be separated from my love (see Romans 8:35–39). *No fear of rejection here.*

You are a brand-new creation in Christ (see 2 Corinthians 5:17). *I made you new and clean on the inside—totally different.*

You are complete in Christ (see Colossians 2:10). *Yep. You have it all . . . love, peace, security, kindness . . .*

You are a saint, a citizen of heaven (see Ephesians 1:1; Philippians 3:20). *This world is not your real home; you are on loan from the throne!*

You have direct access to me (see Ephesians 2:18). *You don't have to use a formula or go through another person!*

You are my workmanship, created for good works (see Ephesians 2:10). *You're my work of art that has been designed to do good things for Jesus!*

You have eternal life in heaven (see 1 John 5:13). *What better place to spend forever?*

You can do all things through Christ who strengthens you (see Philippians 4:13). *What I assign you to do, I will help you through.*

You are free from condemnation (see Romans 8:1–2). *Don't let anyone put you down. I have lifted you up!*

You are protected by my power (see 1 Peter 1:5). *Ask, and I will send my angels anytime!*

Your adequacy comes from me (see 2 Corinthians 3:5). *It is not about what you can do, but about what I can do through you!*

You are sealed in Christ by the Holy Spirit of promise (see Ephesians 1:13). *You are headed to heaven; it's a sure thing!*

You have been given a spirit not of fear, but of power, love, and a sound mind (see 2 Timothy 1:7). *Forget dread, panic, worry, and timidity. You've got the power.*

You are the salt and light in this world (see Matthew 5:13–14). *Your very presence can make others thirsty for me.*

You have been called to bear fruit (see John 15:16). *What joy you have when you see me working in and through you.*

You are seated with Christ in the heavenly realm (see Ephesians 2:6). *You've got spiritual royalty to the max.*

You have been created by me with a plan and purpose in mind (see Jeremiah 29:11–13). *I have your life mapped out.*

You are victorious through Christ (see Romans 8:37). *Victory in Jesus—it's all about obedience.*

You are called to be a witness for Christ and to make disciples (see Mark 16:15; Acts 1:8). *What an honor to tell others about Jesus and help them learn his ways.*

You are filled with my power (see Acts 1:8). *You are never dependent on your own abilities.*

You are crowned with glory and majesty (see Psalm 8:3–5). *You're a prince glowing with my glory!*

What would happen if you started to look at your brother, the guys in youth group, and the Boylanders strutting the halls at school through God's eyes? How would the way you think of or treat a guy change if you saw him from God's point of view? Give it some thought and prayer. ●

Love Letter—From the Heart of a Dad

Karlee and Kali,

When you were both young, we were having a discussion and I asked you what advice I had already given you about boys. Karlee replied, "Dad, you always told me that all boys are dogs." Then Kali looked at me and said, "What's up, dog?"

It's true—all boys are dogs! As you grow and mature, my description of a dog will also change and take on a new meaning. While you were still young and innocent, my advice was that all boys are dogs, that they can be mean and say things and do things that may hurt your feelings. When you were fragile preteens, I reminded you that all boys are dogs and that most of them are not mature enough to be trusted. Now that you are teenagers seeking independence, yet are still very insecure, I will constantly remind you to make good choices, and that all boys are dogs. Boys will say and do anything to get what they want and pressure girls into making bad decisions, decisions they may later regret. All teen boys are dogs, because once they get what they want, they no longer care about you and they no longer want you!

Someday you will meet a guy who will treat you very special and make you feel like a princess. At the time, you will think he is going to be your prince and you will live with him happily ever after. Then he will become a dog and do something stupid that breaks your heart. Each breakup is painful, but one day you will look back and realize that you learned something from each of those relationships. You learned that if a boy really cares about you, he will not say mean things, especially when his friends are around. You learned that if a guy wants your trust, he must earn your trust by always being honest and trustworthy. And perhaps the most important lesson you learned is that if he really cares about you, he will not only tell you, but he will show you that he genuinely cares by respecting you when you do not want to be pressured into doing something you don't want to do—like taking drugs, drinking alcohol, or having sex.

There will only be a few boys in your life whom you can trust and respect, who are good dogs, and one of them is me, your dad. I want you both to know that I will always be here for you, to remind you that you are beautiful and loved, and that . . . all boys are dogs!

Love,
Dad

WHAT TYPE OF GUY IS HE?

The Four
PERSONALITY TYPES

Just like you, guys have been "fearfully and wonderfully made" by God (Psalm 139:14 NIV). They're unique. They're one of a kind (and in some cases, aren't you glad?).

No two guys are exactly alike; however, some have many similarities in their personalities.

Personality is simply the unique blend of character traits and tendencies that makes us who we are! A person's basic personality is inborn. God chooses it. We don't get to put in our order or tell God our preferences. While in our mother's wombs, we weren't given a checklist of traits or a list of people we wanted to be like.

"Oh, God, I want to be bubbly like Joy Williams, or energetic like Stacie Orrico, or giggly like Hilary Duff, or athletic like Laura Wilkinson, or just mysterious or strong or whatever!" Nope, none of that. The God of creation, who started knitting us together from the moment of our conception, intentionally wove and spun certain traits and tendencies that would make each of us—girls and guys—exactly who and what he wanted us to be!

Every guy has an inborn personality. Even those who rarely

speak and rarely change the expression on their faces have personality—that *is* their personality! Some guys naturally like certain things, while other guys dislike them. Some guys are naturally messy, while others are totally organized. Some guys naturally have a kick-back nature, while others seem uptight 99 percent of the time.

For years psychologists and others who study behavior have been observing and analyzing humans. It all started as far back as Hippocrates—that was about four hundred years before Jesus showed up on earth. In fact, Hippocrates was the one who originated the theory that there are four basic personality types. Then, in the 1930s, a man from Norway named Ole Hallesby, who studied theology (theo means God), further developed the four personality types and named them sanguine, choleric, phlegmatic, and melancholy. Yep, it's Greek to you now, but hold on, because I'm going to explain it! These four categories have become popularized once again thanks to Tim LaHaye (the Left Behind series), Florence Littauer (*Getting Along with Almost Anybody*), and

her daughter, Marita.* Florence has added a descriptive word to each of Hallesby's fancy names, which makes them more real to us. They're the popular sanguine, the powerful choleric, the perfect melancholy, and the peaceful phlegmatic. These adjectives more clearly define each type of personality you're about to discover.

Now, how will knowing these crazy-sounding categories help you better understand guys? It won't, unless you study the categories and apply them! But if you do get into it, it will help you know who and what you're dealing with! Gleaning insight into a guy's personality will then help you know how to communicate with him and how he'll communicate with you. And better communication always leads to better understanding.

Personalities Defined

Let's get more specific and go deeper now by defining each of the four types. I will also include some strengths and weaknesses that will give you a fuller picture of each personality.

---

*This little history of the personality types comes from Gary and Carrie Oliver, *Raising Sons and Loving It* (Grand Rapids: Zondervan, 2000), 113.

Popular Sanguine

These dudes are people oriented, spontaneous, and able to tell very expressive (and exaggerated) stories. They have many different types of friends, because they'll talk to anyone and they like everyone to get involved with what they're doing.

They tend to be cheerful, live in the moment, and thrive on being the center of attention.

On the flip side, sunny sanguines can appear selfish, be easily distracted, talk too much (but never to the same degree as a girl), talk too loud, interrupt others, and be childish.

Powerful Choleric

If you need a guy to be in charge of a club, make decisions about the class trip, complete the editing of the school newspaper, or think quick on his feet in an emergency, get a choleric! They're down-to-business dudes. Because of their confidence and self-sufficiency, they don't need a bunch of pals.

On the flip side, they can come off as bossy, stubborn, insensitive, and impatient. They're not natural encouragers and are quite freaked out by the sight of tears. They can be manipulative and demanding and tend to be the last to apologize.

Perfect Melancholy

Need a big boy to figure out a situation, come up with a solution, and then make it happen? The thoughtful, orderly, and detailed melancholy is your man. He has high ideals and willfully sacrifices his time attempting to make things perfect. He makes a loyal and faithful friend.

On the flip side, melancholies care more about schedules and projects than they do about people. Because they have high standards, they easily slide into a funk, at the same time being irritated and resentful at those who don't do stuff right (according to their definition, of course). They naturally dish out criticism, not compliments.

Peaceful Phlegmatic

These Boylanders willingly go with the flow; therefore, they're nice and low-key and fit in easily. They don't get super upset, are rarely stressed, and make great listeners. They can be shy and speak only when spoken to. They're content to just "be."

On the flip side, they hate confrontation, so they'll avoid dealing with issues. They can be slow, lazy mumblers who will never make a decision about anything. They tend to compromise quickly, appearing to have no backbone. They can be boring.

Helpful info, huh? Did certain descriptions start bringing specific guys to your mind? *Oh yeah, Anthony is super organized during science lab and barks at me for not being prepared. I thought he couldn't stand me, but now I see he's a melancholy, and that makes it more okay.*

I noticed that David didn't exactly jump in to help with the homecoming float. I figured he just didn't care about it. But no, he's one of those low-key phlegmatic types.

Josh is so funny and can gather a crowd around himself in a second. He's so obviously that sanguine dude.

A leader who's confident and competitive? That's Nick for sure. What a choleric he is!

Its sorta fun, isn't it? From now on, you'll look at Boylanders in a whole new way! Test yourself. Identify one guy you know who lands in each category:

sanguine ________________

choleric ________________

melancholy ______________

phlegmatic ______________

A Is for Accepted!

Figuring them out just took on a whole new meaning. You'll be trying to peg them from the moment they step within your guy-activated radar. But let me offer a word of warning. Your radar will pick up pure static if you're not sending out accepting vibes. See, a guy, just like you, wants to be accepted for who he is. If you try to force him to be what he's not, forget building a friendship. Forget hanging out with him. Forget getting him to open up and share his thoughts with you. When you purposely (and obviously) try to change him, he'll clam up. Avoid comments like, "Why aren't your more into sports?"

Learn more about the four personalities by checking out Florence Littauer's book *Personality Plus.*

or "I wish you'd just chill and be less intense" or "I can't believe you're an FCA huddle leader—I wouldn't follow you anywhere" or "Being shy is so gay" or "Have you always been so picky?" or "What you just said is totally stupid" or "What are you wearing, geek boy? I need to give you an extreme makeover." Your disapproving comments will shut him down in a second.

Lack of approval mixed with lack of acceptance. Let's see, that would be called . . . **rejection!** Just go ahead and just paste a big *L* on his forehead, 'cause you're making him feel like a loser. The remedy? Keep your mouth shut if you're about to diss him. Not being able to accept him the way he is, is *your* problem, not his. You'll need to pray for the Holy Spirit's help to like and appreciate each guy the way God designed him—inside and out!

> So accept each other just as Christ has accepted you; then God will be glorified.
>
> Romans 15:7 NLT

Quirky Quiz

Forget the guys for a sec and make it all about you. (Temporarily, of course. As B.A.B.E.s, we know that real life is all about God, right?) You need to know your personality type! This will give you insight into yourself—the good, the need for improvement, and the quirky stuff. Let's face it; at some point, we've all been questioned about our personality traits . . .

"Why are you so impatient?" "Why are you so cheerful all the time?" "Why do you like working on projects?" "Who made you the boss?" "Do you always have to have your way?" "When did you realize you were a leader?" "Since when are you Miss Thoughtful?"

We've endured point-blank statements, some that pierce us like arrows, others that pump us up . . .

"You're a great listener." "You're good at making decisions. Will you help me?" "You're so flexible." "You're fun to

Big boys are little boys in larger bodies!

hang out with." "You think you know everything." "You talk too much." "You never remember anything." "You're the queen of holding grudges." "You're such a worrywart."

Knowing your type will help you be okay with others' observations, compliments, or slams. I can hear it now . . .

"How can you be so spontaneous?" "I'm a sanguine!" "A *what*?"

Or, "You seem extra sensitive to other people. Why is that?" "I'm a melancholy!"

Or maybe you'll hear, "You don't seem concerned about this. Don't you care?" "Yeah, I care. I'm just phlegmatic." "A flag maniac? What do flags have to do with anything?"

Think of the interesting conversations you'll have with your girlfriends trying to explain the four categories! But first, it's time to make sure you understand in which category you're strongest. Here are ten incomplete sentences, each having four possible endings. Give four points to the statement that's *most* like you, three points to the statement that's *next most* like you, two points to the statement

that's *next in line*, and one point to the statement that's *least* like you. Go with your first reaction; don't try to analyze everything. Answer as you really are, *not* as you'd like to be!

1. When I'm chilling out with my friends, I . . .

_____ W. love to tell stories
_____ X. What friends? I don't really need friends.
_____ Y. like to listen
_____ Z. go with the flow

2. Most of the time, I'm . . .

_____ W. happy go lucky
_____ X. trying to figure out a solution to a problem
_____ Y. in deep thought
_____ Z. not worried about anything

3. I really like . . .

_____ W. adventure
_____ X. lots of activity
_____ Y. order
_____ Z. peace

4. If something is wrong, I'll . . .

_____ W. make light of it

_____ X. make it right

_____ Y. analyze it

_____ Z. ignore it

5. I'm . . .

_____ W. sorta childlike

_____ X. sorta dramatic

_____ Y. sorta serious

_____ Z. sorta low-key

6. My parents would probably say I . . .

_____ W. don't take things seriously enough

_____ X. am quiet and organized

_____ Y. am often moody

_____ Z. have many different types of friends

7. You can trust me to . . .

_____ W. do things spur of the moment

_____ X. volunteer to be the leader

_____ Y. make everyone feel included

_____ Z. be dependable

8. If I was going on a youth-group trip, I'd volunteer to . . .

_____ W. oversee all the games

_____ X. take charge of planning and purchasing the food

_____ Y. get the exact directions to where we were going

_____ Z. get scholarship donations for people who couldn't afford to go

Scoring: It's simple. Add up all your scores for the Ws, and write the total by the W below. Do the same thing for the Xs, Ys, and Zs. The category with the highest number of points is you!

W (sanguine)   _____
X (choleric)   _____
Y (melancholy) _____
Z (phlegmatic) _____

Go back and review what's been said about that category. Does it fit you like a glove?

Does it describe you pretty well? (Remember, most people are highest in one category but may score in two or three.) Think through your strengths and weaknesses and jot them down.

Strengths: _____

_____

_____

_____

Weaknesses: _____

_____

_____

_____

Did you know that strengths that get way too strong and go over the top can become weaknesses? For instance,

- when the ever-enthusiastic sanguine gets over the top, she can be seen as a big phony exaggerator

- when the confident choleric gets over the top, he can be seen as conceited and stuck-up

- when the perfectionist melancholy gets over the top, she can appear critical and nitpicky

- when the kick-back phlegmatic gets over the top, he tends tend to look irresponsible and lazy

So keep an eye on yourself to be aware when your positive characteristics are about to become not-so-hot qualities! ●

Coed Craziness

Be observant and you'll see Boylanders' personality types, birth orders, and gender differences showing up everywhere. Group settings are best for this. Guys are less intense and more relaxed in groups, giving you the perfect opportunity to get to know them as friends. Try a few of these wacky get-togethers to give the fun a jump start.

Gourmet Ice Cream Tasting! Invite a bunch of girls and guys to meet at the park at a specific time. Show up with a huge bag of ice cream: choose fifteen different flavors. Order one or two scoops (depending on the size of your group), each in a separate cup. Write the flavor on the bottom and a number (one through fifteen) on the side of each cup, get a bunch of tiny spoons from the ice-cream shop, get to the park before your friends, and arrange the ice cream cups on a picnic table in order, one through fifteen (or however many flavors you have). Bring paper and pens so your friends can take a taste from each cup, guess the complete name of the flavor, and write it next to the number on their sheet of paper. Whoever gets the most flavors correct wins! Any ice cream left? Stir it all together to create a giant milkshake! Have small cups available to share the shake. Now get a wild game of volleyball going to burn off those chilly calories!

Pictures Say a Thousand Words! Have your friends dig out their old family photo albums or photo boxes and gather around your kitchen table for a tell-all and tons of laughs. Use the pictures to ask questions so you can learn a ton of new info about each other. Then locate the nearest photo booth in town, pile in, and get a great group shot all squeezed together. No photo booth? Grab a disposable camera, take pix with crazy poses and pyramids, and run it to a one-hour photo shop. In just sixty minutes, you'll have captured new memories on film! Priceless.

Model Madness! Have everyone chip in a few bucks to buy some challenging kits . . . model airplanes, cars, fire trucks, and so on. Then divide into teams and see who can complete their kit the fastest and the best! (Remember, guys like competition, so turning anything into a race will grab their attention.) You could do the same thing using 250-piece puzzles. Go for it!

Expand Your Experiences! Take up a new hobby together. Choose something that's fairly new to everyone so you'll all be beginners. Check the newspaper, the yellow pages, and local craft stores or just ask around to find classes (community programs cost little or nothing at all). You might find a school teacher or church member who excels at something and can give you and your friends private lessons. Cool. Choose from ballroom dancing, golf, cake decorating, painting, or even ceramics.

ADD SOME GROWL, FUR, AND A PAIR OF SHOES

Well-known Christian author and personality Gary Smalley has approached the four personalities in a more playful manner. Instead of using the original names, he switched them to types of animals. This may be more appropriate in dealing with Boylanders! See if you agree!

The popular sanguine is an **otter**. He loves playing around in the water and being the center of attention if he has people watching him from shore. A true show-off!

The powerful choleric is a **lion**. He's to be taken seriously as he prowls around in control of his surroundings making sure all is just right. A born leader!

The perfect melancholy is a **golden retriever**. He's sensitive and loyal, and he cowers down if he thinks anyone is unhappy with him. A perfect pleaser!

The peaceful phlegmatic is a **beaver**. He works hard building things, then hangs out floating around in the water the rest of the day. A dedicated worker!*

*This information on animals as personality types comes from Gary Smalley's book *The DNA of Relationships* (Carol Stream, IL: Tyndale, 2004).

Does imagining the otter, lion, golden retriever, and beaver give you an even clearer picture of the four personality types?

Now let's get a little wacky. If the four categories could be identified by a pair of guy's shoes, what would they be? Match the footwear to the wearer!

checkered sneakers	laid-back beach boy (phlegmatic)
flip-flop sandals	let's-get-the job done guy (choleric)
work boots	happy-go-lucky lad (sanguine)
leather lace-ups	lets-not-miss-a-detail dude (melancholy)

The correct answers would be the lace-ups with the detail dude, the work boots with the get-it-done guy, the flip-flops with the beach boy, and the sneakers with the happy lad. You got them all right, didn't you? You're really catching on to this personality stuff. It's much less puzzling than it was in the beginning, huh?

As I've mentioned, these are generalizations. Most guys will have the majority of characteristics of one category and some of another. They were born that way. What really makes a guy's personality most obvious is when two or three guys in the same family (those would be called brothers) have totally different personalities. For instance, take Prince William and Prince Harry. Prince William shows all the characteristics of a choleric. He comes across as the son who takes charge, takes responsibility, and aims to do the right thing. For instance, after high school graduation (okay, they don't call it high school in the UK), and before he went to Eton College, Windsor, where he studied geography, biology, and history of art, William took a gap year.* He spent time on maneuvers in Belize, working on a farm in the United Kingdom, helping in community projects with other young people in a remote area of Chile, and visiting countries in Africa. Prince Harry, on the other hand, appears to be a classic sanguine with some melancholy mixed in. He wants to have fun and to do life his own way. His adventurous nature took him to Australia and then Africa during his gap year. And the tabloids caught him partying it up a time or two!

Can you imagine William's text message to Harry?

H, what are you thinking? You are useless and undisciplined. Get on with real life, W

---

*Don't get jealous, but in the UK it's traditional to take a year off before going to college or university. Th
is known as a **gap year**! It's a time-out to explore the world, expand your life experiences, and gain a broad
perspective on life. Some people travel, some serve, some work to save money for college. Great idea, huh

Opposites! When you look at these two guys side by side, it's easy to see the differences in their personalities and place them in their respective categories.

These two brothers are also a royal example of the birth-order theory. William is the typical strong leader and outgoing oldest son. Harry proves to be the perfect example of the playful, spoiled youngest son (you'll be happy to know that he's now training in the Royal Military Academy for a career in the army).

If you have brothers, maybe you've seen this in your own family. And it's not just a guy thing. Obviously, you and a sister or you and a bro can have totally different likes and dislikes, traits, and characteristics. Even though you came from the same parents, you still have a God who designed each of you just the way he desired, just the way he intended. We were all created the way we are *on* purpose and *for* a purpose! (For more on this purpose stuff, you gotta read *Girlfriend, You Are a B.A.B.E.!*)

I hope that after looking at the four personality types, you'll conclude that every guy is unique and different. But different isn't wrong; it's God designed. I trust that recognizing a guy's personal characteristics and tendencies will flood you with unreserved understanding of this remarkable species called man! ●

Three Brothers and a Sister: Katie Koerten Tells All When It Comes to a Houseful of Guys!

Growing up with three brothers is quite an adventure. I always played with Ninja Turtles and G.I. Joes instead of Barbies. When it came time for potty training, my brothers taught me how to use the bathroom standing up. Dinner table conversations consisted of sports, sports, and more sports. My girlfriends are always trying to figure out boys, and they have all these misconceptions about them. Luckily for me, living with three brothers has given me insights into the male brain.

First, I've learned that guys don't like asking for help. Something inside them thinks they know everything! My oldest brother, Jonathan, was baking a cake for school. As he mixed the ingredients together, my mom kept asking him if he needed help. He insisted that he knew how to cook. Forty-five minutes later, when the cake came out of the oven, it didn't smell or look like a cake. It started out thick on one end of the pan and then sloped down until there was no cake left on the other side. When he saw the finished product, he blamed the catastrophe on the oven, because after all, he knew how to bake a cake. After my mom asked him a dozen questions about how he'd made the cake, she discovered that he hadn't read any of the directions. Instead of first creaming the butter and then adding the wet and dry ingredients alternately, he'd put everything together in the bowl, stirred it a few times, and poured it in the pan. From this incident, I learned that guys don't like asking for help. They like to do things their own way. We as girls need to understand that. They don't want someone always bugging them about how to do things. Let them learn on their own!

Also, boys approach life very differently than girls do, and shopping is no exception! During the holidays, I went shopping with all three of my brothers. I thought it would be an all-day bonding experience. Little did I know it would be the shortest shopping trip I've ever taken! Jonathan, Brett, and Toby would go in a store, and a minute later they'd be out. They knew what they wanted and wasted no time. And here I was, looking at each piece of clothing, holding it up to my body, and looking in the mirror. Boys go to the mall to conquer. They buy what they need and are ready to leave as soon as possible. Girls, on the other hand, go for the whole experience. We enjoy hanging out with our friends while finding the best bargains at the stores. So next time you ask a guy to go shopping with you and he gives you a weird look, don't take it personally. He probably likes you—he just doesn't like the mall! Also, the way guys view shopping is how they view a lot of things. They like to be straight to the point. For example, when you're talking to a guy, he doesn't want you going on and on about your problems. Say what's necessary and leave it at that.

Lastly, living with three brothers has allowed me to realize that boys are wired differently emotionally. Even at an early age, I noticed this distinction. When I was five years old, we put a nativity outside our house at Christmastime. Early on Christmas morning, my brothers and I went outside in our pajamas to tell baby Jesus happy birthday. We went over to the wooden manger, laid presents down, and then began to worship him. I worshiped baby Jesus by holding him gently in my arms and kissing his forehead. My brothers, on the other hand, worshiped him by break dancing around the manger, singing songs at the top of their lungs, and just going wild! Both forms of worship were acceptable, but they were completely different. Girls are sweet and caring. We're emotionally bonded to many things, because we were born with that nurturing spirit. Boys, however, enjoy action and excitement. They don't express themselves the same way we do.

Oh, the joys of living in a house full of boys! I'm thankful that God gave me three great brothers who have taught me a lot and helped me through life. Boys can be quite confusing, so don't worry if you don't understand them all the time. God made girls and guys so different . . . and that's what's so awesome!

atie Koerten is surrounded by guys—her brothers! ne recently graduated valedictorian of her senior ass and delivered an inspirational graduation eech—just as her bros did. She was a *Brio* Girl 05 top four finalist, and she has the coolest rapbooks ever!

Love Letter—From the Heart of a Dad

Lydia and Melinda:

There's no time like the present for me to share with you some things that have weighed on my heart and mind ever since the first day I saw your faces. These things are hard for me to share with you, for they are the kinds of things that tend to make me blush and make you giggle. Nonetheless, they are words that I hope will work their way into the deepest recesses of your hearts and minds and grow into the full bloom of wisdom.

I want to talk with you about your husbands. Even writing the word makes me cringe a little, bringing up in my soul both the most protective and most hopeful of emotions. One of my greatest desires for you in life is for each of you to find, even when you least expect it, the man God has in mind for you to marry. At the same time, I want to offer you some strong advice about how to tell the good qualities from the potentially bad ones in the guys who come your way.

The kind of guy I wish upon you, for which I pray, will first be a man who loves Jesus even more than he loves you. If you are at the pinnacle of a guy's devotion, then Jesus is in the wrong place in his heart. When this happens, it will always be possible that someday you will be in the wrong place in his heart. A man who will give up anything and everything to follow Jesus is a man who will give up almost anything and everything to love and keep you.

I also want you to take notice of a man who will treat everyone around him with respect. I have had the displeasure of knowing young men who have been full of courtesy when in the presence of parents and other adults but who despise and ridicule them when they are absent. You want someone who genuinely values the relationships he has with everyone. This is particularly true when it comes to the way he relates to your mom and me—if he is as polite, respectful, and humorous away from us as he is with us, he demonstrates a consistent character. He just might be a "keeper."

Remember, too, that you want to find a guy who is as interested in your heart and mind as he is in your body. I can hear what you're thinking as you read this: "Oh, Dad!" However, this is an important distinction as you learn to relate to the opposite sex. The younger they are, the more apt they will be to focus on warm kisses and warmer embraces. If that is all he is interested in, or if he expresses some sense of entitlement to it after focusing on your heart and mind the rest of the day, then reconsider whether or not you should be around him. Your sexual purity belongs to you alone. Sexual chemistry is one of God's best gifts to humanity, but it is intended to help define attraction before marriage and define the intimacy of that relationship only after marriage. He needs to love the whole you.

Bear with me as I offer just a couple more pieces of advice. I would like you to understand that guys think differently than girls do. This may be a "duh" moment for you, but let me clarify what I mean. Boys naturally focus on life in different ways than girls do. While it may be an overgeneralization, most guys tend to focus on task more than relationship, listen to reason more than emotion, and respond more to challenges than to gentle encouragement. While the rough edges of these natural responses may smooth out over the years, they will never disappear. A teen guy you meet now will keep most of who he is as he matures. Is he easily angered now? He will have trouble with that in the future. Is he passionate now? Count on experiencing that in the decades ahead. Is he lazy? He'll likely be as attached to the couch at forty as he is at eighteen. Think deeply about the behaviors and attitudes he now displays, and consider whether or not that's what you want to live with in years to come.

Finally, let me selfishly remind you of what I have told you at every stage of your personal and emotional growth: your mother and I will always be your parents. That means that you can expect us to be as interested and as helpful as we have always been. Speaking for myself, this means that I will always tend toward protecting you, seeing suspicious motives in the guys who walk into our home and into your heart. It means that I will always expect a lot out of you, that you must never give up your dreams, your manners, or your faith. And it means that you can count on me for impassioned advice, whether or not you ask for it.

I will simply end by telling you that I love you and I want you to be loved by a man who loves you even more than do I. God is preparing him for you even now. I'll be saving up for your wedding.

All my love,
Dad

HEY, NOW YOU'RE SPEAKING MY LANGUAGE!

GET HIM TALKING

Mastering the Art of Conversation

It's true that everything that's worthwhile takes time, takes practice, takes patience. Mastering the art of conversation is one of these things. Learn it, eat it, sleep it, breathe it! You'll see the benefits forever—and not only in your relationships with guys, but also in your relationships with girlfriends, parents, employers, you name it. This communication stuff will improve your life as you get to know others and develop meaningful bonds.

Talk, talk, talk. Yack, yack, yack. Chat it up! Girls adore the spoken word. Even girls who are innies (introverts) by nature enjoy a good blab session with a friend. You may have the gift of gab, but that doesn't automatically qualify you as a true conversationalist. Conversation involves connection. It isn't one-sided chatter. Real conversation isn't dominated by one person. It requires two (or more) people talking—but not at the same time! It's a back and forth thing. She talks; he talks. It's sorta like a tennis match. The back-and-forth action makes it a true game with balance that's enjoyed by both participants! If not, the one getting pelted with hard yellow rubber balls isn't having fun. Sure, the one doing the pelting is having a blast. The same is true for conversations. If one person—the girl—is dominating, the other person—the guy—feels

Start a conversation with an introduction—*yours*! Say your name, share something about yourself, then ask his name. "Hey, I'm Amy. I've played soccer on this field forever. What about you?" If it sounds too cheesy for you, then go ahead—just sit there.

like he's being pelted with words. Not fun. So both people being in the game is *good*. Back and forth, one at a time (otherwise, it's noisy chaos).

Connecting is key in conversation, in communication, and in building friendship. Conversation helps you get to know a guy better, which naturally helps you to understand him better.

Tongue-Tied

If you clam up the second you step into Boyland, this will help. The way to start a conversation is to **ask questions**. Begin with nonthreatening (don't put the guy on the spot), easy-to-answer questions that basically have a yes or no answer. They're great starter questions, especially when you've just met the guy.

Yes or no questions:

Did you have fun at the football game?

Have you ever had a skinny mocha latte?

Are you going on the youth group ski trip?

Do you have any brothers or sisters?

Do you think that pop quiz was hard?

Add your own:

_____

_____

_____

_____

Next, try a few fact-finding questions. Again these don't require much personal information or thought from the guy, since they're still surface-level questions.

Fact-finding questions:

Where did you grow up?

Who's your favorite NFL team?

What's the best gift you've ever received?

When did you start your relationship with God?

What teacher do you want for biology next year?

What band are you into?

What was hardest part for you to understand about that book we read in English?

Add your own:

_____

_____

_____

_____

Want to get to know him? Find common ground (things you're both interested in) and build from there.

Now it's time to move to open-ended questions. These questions usually require more than a simple answer. They encourage the guy to identify and then share his opinions, his thoughts, his ideas, and possibly his hopes or inner feelings. If you learn how to do this, you'll hit the jackpot.

Open-ended questions:

If you were the principal, why would you close the campus during lunch period?

How do you deal with it when your parents make you angry?

When do you think Jesus will come back?

What do you think our nation would be like if we had a woman president?

What do you think about changing the school's fight song?

What's it like being the yearbook editor?

What do you want to be doing ten years from now?

Add your own:

_____

_____

_____

_____

It's absolutely essential, unbelievably important, that when a guy shares stuff in response to these deeper questions, you handle it with TLC. It's here that you can blow it by making a snide remark or belittling him—and turn him into an *ice man*. He'll freeze up, shut down, lock the door to his soul, and throw away the key! Okay, maybe it won't be that drastic in every case, but this is very important. You may not agree with his opinions or ideas, but don't slam him or you'll lose your chance to really know what's going on in his head and heart.

I think that moving strategically through this Q & A stuff with guys is huge. Remember how we learned that they aren't hip to girls yapping on and on? Remember, they're wired to be less talkative, less emotional. Use this information! Talk back and forth. Don't push for answers—in fact, if he doesn't really answer, let it go! Once you've developed a tight friendship with a guy, you can move more quickly to the open-ended questions.

The benefits of connectedness, feeling valued, being accepted, and having someone who likes you and cares about you are all worth the effort of mastering the art of conversation. It's worth it for you and for your guy friend.

> **If you quickly jump topics on a guy, you might lose him, and you might overwhelm him. Remember, he's a waffle! Let him close one box before he opens another. It might be helpful to say, "Okay, new subject," just so he knows you're about to change direction!**

Becoming an Active Listener

Fact: The average person can listen five times faster than he or she can talk. So let's say you can listen to 400 words a minute but the guy is talking about 120 words a minute. What's your brain doing with the extra time? If one person is talking, what should the other person be doing? If the guy is actually talking to you, what should *you* be doing? Gliding on some lip gloss, watching TV, scanning radio stations, answering your cell phone, or picking off your

old fingernail polish are all *wrong* answers. You should be listening!
Listening is an *action* word. It involves concentration, eye contact,
and thought about what the guy is saying! Listening is the key in
this conversation challenge. Listening is vital in making a connection! You can be a good *and active* listener!

Here are some tips:

- Don't interrupt. It's rude and proves you aren't really hearing
  the guy out.
- Look at the guy who's talking to you—especially his eyes.
  Some guys are uncomfortable or insecure about having eye
  contact until they're super comfortable with you. Don't take
  it personally if he isn't glued to you at first. As your friendship
  deepens, he should feel confident about looking directly at
  you.
- Prove you're listening by showing responses as he shares: nodding and using comments like, "Oh!" "Really?" "Uh-huh."
- Ask questions that show you're hearing him: "Then what?"
  "How did you respond?" "What would you have done differently?" Obviously, the question has to match the conversation. If your friend just unloaded about the fights going on
  between his parents and you say, "What would you have
  done differently?" it will be glaringly obvious that you were
  off in never-never land. He wasn't talking about himself! And
  asking, "Do they have the TV on when they argue?" shows
  you're totally missing what he's saying. Listening involves
  concentration, so concentrate!
- No matter how tempted you are, don't interrupt. Guys resent
  this.
- Be empathetic (try to imagine yourself in the guy's situation and see it from his point of view). This will help you
  understand.

> "He who answers a matter before he hears the facts—it is folly and shame to him." Proverbs 18:13 AMP

- Don't plan what you're going to say back to the guy while he's still talking. It disconnects your brain from what he's saying.
- Engage your brain by listening for key words and phrases like *feel, think, if only.*
- Hear what the guy is *not* saying. Don't make assumptions or put words in his mouth.
- Check out his body. Um, body language, that is! The way a person sits, slumps, leans, folds his arms—all of it communicates a message.
- Did I mention that you really, really, really shouldn't interrupt?

B.A.B.E., when you've tossed the conversation back and forth using active listening skills, the guy will feel like he has connected with you. He'll feel like you care. He'll begin to trust you. And vice versa. Having this type of relationship with a guy far outweighs having a string of romantic escapades that end in a broken heart. Trust me. ●

Since guys are easily overwhelmed by a girl's gift of gab, don't expect them to automatically lend you a listening ear. Instead, ask for permission to spill!

"I'd like to tell you about _____. Are you up for it?"
"Want to hear the funniest story ever about _____?"
"I just had the biggest fight with _____. Feel like listening?"

When he mentally commits to listening, he'll make the effort to do it.

Layers
of
communication

In my late teens, I was introduced to the idea of levels or layers of communication. Today we could call it the *Shrek* analogy (yep, from the movie). Shrek explains to Donkey that ogres are like onions— they have layers—and their layers have to be slowly peeled away with trust and confidence in the genuine nature of the relationship. Well, guys are like ogres—I didn't say they *were* ogres (you'll have to decide that on your own). They have layers. In his classic book, *Why Am I Afraid to Tell You Who I Am?* John Powell shares that we communicate on at least five different levels, or in *Shrek* talk, layers. This applies to our communication with our girlfriends and parents as well as guys. Let's start with the outer layer—cliché.

Layer Five: Cliché Conversation

This is very safe talk that doesn't require any personal sharing. It's all about small talk: "Hey, what's up?" "I like your haircut." It's surface level and nonconfrontational.

Layer Four: Reporting the Facts about Others

This is where you talk about other people or things that are happening at school or in the world but don't say anything about your personal opinion on the topics discussed.

Layer Three: My Ideas and Judgments

Ooh, this layer may hesitate to peel off. The guy is testing the waters—Are you for real? Can you be trusted? He steps out to share his ideas and thoughts. How will you respond? Believe me, he's watching and waiting. He's also tuned in to whether or not you go blab his business to your friends. If you do, he's not going to level one or two with you.

Layer Two: My Feelings or Emotions

This is where it gets good. You know the guy thinks highly of you as a friend if he's willing to talk about the way he *feels* about the facts and ideas he's shared. When he reveals emotions (other than anger, which guys show easily), a major layer is coming off. Keep in mind that most guys aren't super comfortable with their emotions. They're thinkers by nature—we're the more emotional ones. Trust has to be there!

Layer One: Complete Emotional and Personal Truthful Communication

This layer doesn't come off very often for most guys. It's rare. Some of them don't even know they *have* this layer! It's deep. It's right at the core. When it's peeled off, guys feel extremely vulnerable —like, emotionally naked. This layer requires total openness, trust, and complete honesty. Some friendships may not get here. But the friendship you eventually take into marriage will be most fulfilling for you as a woman if you get to this layer on the really important issues.

Interesting, huh? Do you know what helps you start moving through these layers of communication? Asking questions! Great, you know all about that—we just covered it. You're gaining the tools and skills you need to unlock guys and really get to know them.

News flash: Ever get frustrated when you share at layer two and the guy responds at layer five? Girl: "I've really been praying about my bitterness toward my mom. I feel guilty about it. But sometimes I get so crazy mad around her that I'm actually thinking about living with my grandparents. What do you think I should do?" Guy: "If they have a pool, then that would be cool to live with them."

We communicate at the level of our layers! Girls typically like to go deeper; guys don't. Just don't be pushy or judgmental. Be gentle and patient, and you might get a glimpse of a new layer!

Want to get him to open up? Get active! Guys are more likely to share if they're doing an activity they enjoy and feel comfortable doing (fishing, shooting hoops, driving, jogging, hiking, and eating are a few).

The Big Squeeze:
Andrea Taylor Spills Her Thoughts on Hugging!

I sat on a rock wall near the exit of one of the rides at a local theme park, waiting for a few girls from my youth group to emerge from the ride. As I sat, I watched people. Beyond the rock wall across the road from my perch, hundreds of people stood in line for a new ride, which promised to rocket them from zero to fifty in less than three seconds. Some looked nervous, others excited. (I also saw two kids walk by eating a huge chocolate-chip cookie, and I wanted to ask them for a bite but decided against it.) As I watched, my attention was drawn to a single girl. She wore a pink T-shirt and blue jeans. On her shirt, a sign attached with safety pins read, "Free Hugs." I thought the sign looked interesting and that she was a brave girl to be standing alone with such a sign. Soon, however, I learned she wasn't alone. More girls appeared with the same sign. I felt like the place where I was sitting was being invaded by the Hug Squad. I wanted to run, not because I was scared of the girls, but because I have issues with hugs.

Hugs seem to be everywhere. People are always hugging in movies, at the airport, at family reunions, and every place imaginable. Even Hershey's makes a candy called Hugs. Yet despite the gesture's popularity, I began to wonder, *Is there such a thing as proper hugging etiquette?* I investigated.

It's my duty as a B.A.B.E. to share with you, also a B.A.B.E., three keys to proper hugging etiquette. The first key is to prepare by warming up (okay, I made this part up, but it's totally sensible). Nobody wants a wimpy hug, nor does anyone want to have to rush you to the hospital because you strained a muscle. Therefore, it's necessary to warm up your muscles before you begin hugging. Three basic warm-up techniques exist. The first technique is to roll your shoulders. Rolling your shoulders gets your muscles relaxed and ready. This allows you to stretch your arms and pull someone into your embrace. It also allows you to hold someone tightly. The next warm-up technique is to roll your wrists. Rolling your wrists prepares them for that very special one-two-three tap. The one-two-three tap is important when you want to let your huggee (the person you're hugging) know you really love him or her, because each tap stands for a word. The first tap represents *I*. The second tap represents *love*. And the third tap? You guessed it—*you*. (You use the tap when you're holding someone in an embrace and you decide to pat his or her back three times. Ever notice that? Not one, not six, but three taps.) The final warm-up technique is the self-hug. The self-hug allows you to practice the one-two-three tap and can help you become more aware of how you yourself prefer to be hugged. For example, you can try hugging yourself tightly; just wrap your arms around yourself and squeeze with all your might. You can also try a weaker hug by loosening your squeeze. After determining the strength of hug you prefer, you can be better prepared for how you hug another person or how you want to react to another person's hug. Your reaction may help the person determine how to better hug you in the future. Let's review the three warm-up techniques before moving on. First, roll your shoulders; second, roll your wrists; and third, hug yourself. Now that you know how to prepare for hugging, let's look at the second key to proper hugging etiquette: style! Let's look at four of the more popular styles.

The Bone-Crushing Bear. This hug comes with a buyer-beware label, because if you opt to use this hug, you may hurt someone. This hug consists of grabbing huggees before they can react to you. You pin the huggees' arms to their sides, causing them to be unable to return the hug; therefore, if you're looking for a shared hug, this hug isn't suggested.

The Mushy-Gushy. This hug requires both the huggee and the hugger to play equal rolls. In other words, both members must share in the embrace. Both parties hug each other tightly, with full-body contact. (To make the mushy-gushy hug absolutely perfect, have soft music playing in the background.) Romantic companions may seem like the most obvious people for this type of embrace, but friends can hug each other this way too—just forego the soft music and lighten up on the full-body contact. (Unless you're married to the huggee, it's best to forego the full-body contact altogether in guy-girl hugs—a guy might get the wrong idea!)

The Side-by-Side. This hug is found in many Kodak moments and is a sweet and innocent way to show someone you care. It's safe (no crushing, no mush), and it's the least *misunderstood* hug (let's be frank—if you use the mushy-gushy hug with a guy, he may assume you have a thing for him). The side-by-side hug speaks of fondness and friendship. This is the best hug between girls and guys.

The A-Frame. This hug needs both parties to participate. They both lean forward with the top half of their bodies, touching only at the shoulder. It's sort of a modified version of the bone-crushing bear, except way more delicate. It's frontal but not full body! To be sure it doesn't become full body, simply lift your hand up in front of your chest, palm facing out, and lightly touch (or push when necessary) the person to let him know your intentions.

Once you're familiar with these styles, you should also become familiar with *when* these styles are most appropriate. For example, the bone-crushing bear hug is most appropriate with friends and relatives—people you know extremely well. The mushy-gushy hug is most appropriate between people who are truly in love (and best if they're married), because it can invoke a physical stimulation in both parties (more on this coming up). The A-frame hug is great for friends, because both parties participate but you don't smash your whole body against someone else's. Finally, the side-by-side hug is appropriate in almost any setting, because it allows two people to show affection without committing to a full-body embrace. One should always use the most appropriate style when hugging another.

This brings us to the third key in proper hugging etiquette. If you're going to hug, do it with pure intentions. This is important. Hugging can be a very intimate action, especially between teenage girls and guys. Sometimes we as young women don't realize the impact our hugs can have on guys (and especially guys trying to live for Christ). The feeling of our bodies against theirs can cause their minds and hearts to be led astray. *Oh, happy day, her breasts are touching my chest! This would be awesome skin on skin. I wonder if she'd be willing to* . . . And on from there! The warmth of a girl's body against a guy's can easily trigger sexual thoughts. Our bodies against theirs can lead them to a place far from pure. Girls, admit it, we can be just the same, yet we vary in our responses. Some girls *want* their body smashed up against a guy's; they want to turn him on like a big tease. They hug a bit tighter or longer hoping he'll catch the drift. Other girls suddenly see themselves walking down that church aisle in the most awesome white wedding dress.

See, hugging isn't just about a hug. It's about purity.

Once a guy's or girl's mind thinks beyond the hug, it's prone to fantasy and lust. The Bible tells us that lusting is impure. God has called us to be pure and to be holy (1 Thessalonians 4:7). Spend time in prayer about it. You may decide to hug guys only side by side. Or you may decide that hugging isn't such a great idea. You may decide that when a hug is offered, you'll return it with a high five or a handshake. You may decide that choosing not to be all huggy serves a greater purpose, one that leads toward purity of mind and body.

"If you call out for insight and cry aloud for understanding. . . . Then you will understand what is right and just and fair—every good path" (Proverbs 2:3, 9 NIV).

Andrea Taylor, *Brio* Girl 2003, is a student at Southwest Baptist University majoring in communications. She loves missions, little kids' laughter, and hugging—her dad! She's saving her lovin' arms for God's guy for her.

Back Talk

No, no, no! This kind of talking back isn't about sassing someone. This kind of back talk has to do with helping you understand the message and the meaning of your conversations with guys. Many girls tell me that after chatting with a guy, they don't have clue what he was talking about or what he meant by what he said! Some guys struggle with saying what they're thinking.

It's very easy for messages to get mixed up. No wonder we misunderstand each other! What we say, what we think we said, what we meant to say, and what they heard might not be close at all! It's like sitting in a circle playing that telephone game when you were a kid. "Shawna and Steve sat side by side on the seashore at sunset" mutates its way to "Should a beve be seeda see a horse knit." That makes absolutely no sense. Yet that's exactly the way we can feel about a brief exchange or a lengthy (yeah, right) talk with guys. So this simple technique will, hopefully (I can't promise 100 percent success when dealing with Boylanders), clarify for you (and probably for him) what he's saying. It's a proven method that has been around forever. So listen up—you're about to be enlightened.

A guy makes a statement: "I can't believe I always say something stupid when Priscilla is around. She must hate me."

You repeat it back to him: "You think Priscilla hates you because you say stupid stuff around her?"

He clarifies: "Yes, dumb things fly out of my mouth when she steps within twenty feet of me."

Or you get it wrong, and he corrects you:

You say, "You hate being around Priscilla? You shouldn't really call her stupid."

He says, "No, I say stupid things, and I'm afraid she hates me."

Simple. But it takes practice! The effort has a great payoff. It will increase the percentage you comprehend of what the guy is saying and what he means by what he says. This boosts your communication, which in turn boosts your understanding. And right now we're all about learning to understand guys. That's why you picked up this book! ●

THE FORGIVENESS FACTOR

I want to point out that sometimes guys will say and do things they *don't* mean. Imagine that! A guy may tell you he'll definitely be at your volleyball game, and then he won't show. He might say he doesn't like so-and-so, and then he'll turn around and ask her to the dance. Other times guys *do* mean to do what they do! A guy could make you the target of a cruel joke in front of his friends. He may uninvite you to a day of waterskiing at the lake. Are you feeling the pain?

There's no way around it. Guys *will* do stuff that hurts you. If a guy is your friend, then he probably isn't doing it on purpose, meaning it isn't premeditated, preplanned, calculated evil! It just turns out that way, or at least it seems that way to you. So for your friendship to be lasting and free from bitterness buildup, you'll need to scrub your heart with a powerful agent known as **forgiveness**. This isn't an option, B.A.B.E.! It's a requirement.

Krista, a girl in my small group, shared this:

When I was a junior, Todd was one of my good friends. We made plans to go on the class trip together—to sit together, to swap CDs—that kind of stuff. Two weekends before the trip, he fell for this girl, Lynn. Without telling me, he arranged for her to be with him on the class trip. When I got to the bus, they were already sitting together. My heart sank, and I went straight into a fog. It took a while, but I had to forgive him; otherwise, it would have been the end of a really great three-year friendship.

You may not think you have it in you to forgive, but you do! You have the Holy Spirit, that bit of God living in you, making you a divine diva. He will strengthen you to forgive. You don't even have to feel like it. Forgiveness is an act of your will. Your will or choice to forgive, followed up by your actions, will release the flow of forgiveness in your heart toward the guy. Eventually that forgiveness will be replaced by Holy Spirit love. That love is *in* your heart. Here's proof:

> But the fruit [natural by-product of the Spirit living in you] of the Spirit is love.
>
> Galatians 5:22 NIV

> The love of God is shed abroad in our hearts by the Holy Ghost which is given unto us.
>
> Romans 5:5 KJV

Choose forgiveness. Then act on it. This is a tough must-do. You must treat the guy like you've let it go, like you've forgiven him. If you give him the cold shoulder, refusing to acknowledge his presence, you haven't forgiven him. Don't play games with yourself. True forgiveness places the guy back where he was (in your heart and life) before he hurt you. You definitely need Spirit power to do this—but you *have it*!

When you're struggling with the forgiveness issue, remember this. *You* have been forgiven by your heavenly Father, through Jesus, for what you've done wrong. How could you withhold that from someone else? You can't. Your forgiveness can't be dependent on whether or not you think the guy *deserves* it. You can forgive with God's help. ●

"Bear with each other and forgive whatever grievances you may have against one another. Forgive as the Lord forgace you." Colossians 3:13 NIV

Love Letter—From the Heart of a Dad

My daughter Megan,

I hope it is okay for me to call you that. You are indeed my flesh and blood, my daughter. Yet I worry that since I haven't been around for you, you won't want me to claim you as mine and you won't want to claim me either.

I know that over the years, you have tried to figure out why I left. I hope you can someday understand that it wasn't because of you. The blame goes to me. I truly do regret that day I drove away, watching you in my rearview mirror. It is an image that has haunted me. I never wanted to hurt you (or your mom). I truly didn't want you to pay the price for my decision to walk away. But I know that's what has happened. You have needed me, and I have not been there.

That's why I'm writing. See, I fear that you're seeking from others—especially guys—the love and attention that I have not given you.

I've heard that you've dated a lot—had lots of guys, sorta one after the other. I've heard about the revealing clothes you wear (your uncle told me he saw you at the mall). People have said that girls do this when they have been pushed away or abandoned by their dads. This is hard for me to say, but if you are going to try to look for the love that I did not give you, please look to the One who made you. Look to God. He knows each hurt, each hole, each heavy thought. And he is the only one who knows how to fill up the empty places inside of you, places that are there because of me. I can imagine you laughing right now, saying, "Oh, nice time to offer fatherly advice."

But I know God can mend anything. I know that's true, because I gave my life to him three years ago. He has been mending me ever since.

I know I don't deserve it, but I have to ask you this one question. Will you forgive me? Is it possible? I know I've screwed up, but I want to make it right, if you will let me. I know I can't make up for the hurt I've caused, but if we both look to God, I believe we can move forward from here. I will be watching the mail for your response. I pray you will believe that even though I have not been around, I have not stopped loving you.

Dad

Communication Commitment

So how are you doing with all the stuff we've chatted about? You've learned lots of new info and ideas. Do you have a better understanding of Boylanders? Just to make sure you're tracking with me, let's do this.

Review section 6, then answer the following statements T for true, F for—well, you know!

_____ Guys always say exactly what they mean.
_____ Generally, guys are in touch with their deepest emotions.
_____ The purpose of conversation is to connect with the other person.
_____ You may love to talk, but most guys have a hard time paying attention if you ramble on and on.
_____ Drop hints! Guys are experts at picking up on them.
_____ You must be direct with guys, saying what you mean or what you want.
_____ Guys can read your mind.
_____ True conversation is like tennis—it goes back and forth, with both people participating.
_____ Conversation is an art that takes practice.
_____ Open-ended questions can be answered with a simple yes or no.
_____ You can listen faster than you can talk.
_____ Being super critical will cause a guy to clam up.
_____ When he talks, you listen.
_____ There are fifty-five basic layers of communication.
_____ Full-body hugs should be given to anyone, at any time.
_____ Back talk means to repeat back to the guy what you're hearing him say.
_____ Even though you've been hurt, guys are worth forgiving.

You're getting wise to the ways of communicating with the opposite sex. Yet here's the thing. Gaining knowledge is great, but it's only half of what you need. Putting it into action is the other half. Just like with anything, knowing *how* to do something and actually doing it are two different things.

Are you ready and willing to commit to doing the things we've talked about so you can communicate with and understand guys better? See, it's not just about the guy; it's about you too. Commit, practice, and persevere! Make your commitment here:

I, _____, am ready and willing to put the required effort into developing the art of communication. In doing so, I will understand guys, and myself, much better.

Signature: _____

Date: _____

You realize this communication stuff can be used to improve *all* your relationships—mom, dad, siblings, best girlfriend—right?

Answers: F, T, T, F, T, F, T, T, F, T, T, F, F, T

THE ULTIMATE GOAL . . . FRIENDSHIP!

The Equation

According to Barb and Gary Rosberg, known as America's Family Coaches, one of the top needs for the male gender is *companionship*. What do you think of when you hear that word? Someone to hang out with, to go to the movies with, to be there when you need to spill what's on your mind? All of these are correct. Companionship can be defined as friendship. Guys need the friendships of girls.

This is how the equation goes:

Embracing his differences + Engaging him in conversation = Fulfilling friendships

Let's break it down.

First, recognize that guys are different than we are and be okay with it—even celebrate it. Add to that your new skills for having tight conversations and spending time doing things together in groups, which allows you to get to know each other without romantic tension. What do you get? Fulfilling friendship. And that's exactly what guys need. I admit that lots of them think they need some hottie who is willing to satisfy their bodies' sexual desires, but in their heart of hearts, friends rank high. Friends are remembered and valued. Friends are still in the picture years down the road.

Guys Need Girls as Friends

Let's look at some of the reasons guys need girls as friends:

- You can support them in their activities and schoolwork.
- You can applaud their decisions to live for God.
- You can cheer them on when they choose to do the right thing.
- You can allow them to be more genuine and real without the stress of typical guy-to-guy ridicule or teasing.
- You can boost their self-esteem (the way they feel about themselves) and self-confidence.
- You're easier to talk to than guys, which helps them talk out situations or relationship blues with you.
- You can give them a girl's point of view.
- They can relax and be themselves when there's no romantic tension (this works to your advantage, since you'll get to see who they really are and what they're all about).
- You can remind them who they are in Christ when they get down on themselves or their guy friends trash them.
- Authentic interaction with girls allows guys to see that lasting relationships are built on solid friendships.

Add yours here:

_____

_____

_____

_____

Girls Need Guys as Friends

You might get caught up in the wicked web of twisted thinking that you need a hot hunk of a guy to make your existence meaning-

Are your relationships with Boylanders platonic? If they're close-knit but lacking the cuddly, caressing stuff, the answer is *yes*!

ful. **Snap out of it!** Soap operas and fairy tales are not true! The ways of this world are twisted. First and foremost, you need guys as friends. Why? Check it out.

- They can help you get a clearer understanding of how guys think, act, and feel differently than girls do—this is key to knowing how to respond to them!
- They can give you a guy's point of view.
- They can help in your conflicts with girls by looking at the situation with less emotion and without taking everything so personally.
- They can help you develop your listening skills.
- They can help you truly understand that lasting relationships are built on solid friendships.
- They can encourage you and support you in "guy" ways.
- They can give you insight into Boyland.
- They can protect you (they do this naturally, since God built them with this instinct).
- They can defend you and stick up for you when other guys are being jerks.

"'Don't expect me to stay on the phone forever or to text you fifteen times a day. That's what I would like to say to girls if I had a chance." Randy, 15

- They can allow you to relax and be your true self because there's no romantic tension.

Add yours here:

_____

_____

_____

_____

"The key to appreciating guys is to focus on their strengths—look for them. For instance, guys are good at handling crisis. They have the ability to shut down their emotions and deal with the problem at hand. Sometimes we want them to be more emotional! But we can either get upset at the trait, or we can remember how valuable it is when crisis hits. Choose to applaud guys for this trait, and others, instead of seeing the down side." Pam Farrel

"Girls shouldn't put themselves down or ask dumb questions like, 'Do I look fat in this?' There's no way a guy can answer that question without a girl getting upset—no matter how you answer, she won't believe you." Kurt, 18

Girls and Girlfriends, Guys and Guy Friends

Because of the differences in the sexes, it's incredibly important that girls have girlfriends and guys have guy friends. If a girl hangs out only with a group of guys or a guy is forever tagging along with a group of girls, something somewhere is out of balance.

Girls, don't be wishy-washy, fair-weather friends. You know the type—they're the kind who love your company as long as there's not a guy around. Dropping your girlfriends as quickly as a boy comes around is rude, immature, selfish, and unhealthy. Besides, guys are limiting. I mean, come on. They don't really want to hit the mall to try on every perfume as you search for your new scent. They're easily bored hearing every single detail of your life. Girlfriends love to listen to you blab and are always up for the mall, a gooey sundae, or a chick flick.

Plus, our girlfriends are more likely to be honest with us about life stuff. They aren't so afraid you'll hate them for telling you what's real.

Guys need to spend time with their guy friends—they've got some grunting and hunting to do that girls just don't get! Some girls try to fit in and act more like guys. Not so good. Let the boys be boys. Recently on a mission trip, I listened by the door to the guys' room (don't tell them). They would tell jokes and laugh like hyenas; then one of them would rip a big one, and they'd all fall over laughing again. Throw a girl into the mix, and the dynamics change. It's just a fact. That's not to say they won't fart in front of you—the impolite ones will. But it's just the same with a group of girls—add a guy, and the outcome is different.

Guy friends are wonderful, but, B.A.B.E.s, girlfriends are a must!

Flirting with
FLIRTING

Do real friends flirt? My personal experience tells me no. Here's why.

My freshman year of high school, I was crushin' bad on this guy in my homeroom—we'll call him Eric. He had dishwater blond hair and broad shoulders, and he walked like a jock.

That, of course, was because he was a jock! Starting on both the varsity football and basketball teams, he was the BMOC (big man on campus) of my high school, and of my heart. Truth be told, he was my single motivation for attending sporting events!

I was so excited that I was assigned to sit kitty-corner from him in homeroom so I could always see him out of the corner of my eye. That way I could stare at him without him knowing —but you'd already figured that out, huh? It was perfect. And may I point out that this is the best and only acceptable way to stare!

Entering homeroom each morning and walking by him, I'd smile and squeak out a "Hi, Eric" (back then you didn't say "hey"). He'd give me the coolest nod and say, "Hi, Andrea, how ya doing?" That's when my brain would chill from the thrill and I wouldn't be able to think of a *thing* to say!

Pouring on the charm wasn't one of my specialties. Having cutesy comebacks or fluttering lashes wasn't me. I knew some girls who were great flirts. They would use their eyes, their shoulders, their faces, their bodies—all to grab the attention of their targets.

If flirting was an Olympic event, they would win the gold!

I would've never medaled!

Now, this is the good part. When I was a sophomore, one of Eric's friends liked my sister, so he and Eric would come over to hang out. We'd shoot pool, play ping-pong, and eat tons of frozen pizzas. And during that time, I got to know Eric. I got to know the pressure he was under to perform well at his sports and his grueling efforts to maintain his grades. I got to know what was going on in his family. He opened up about his parents' divorce and how he missed his dad. (And I got to know that he wasn't very good at pool!)

I didn't flirt with Eric.

I never did have a date with him (all those wasted daydreams)!

But I learned something valuable: being real far outweighs being flirty.

See, when Eric had a problem he needed to talk out or a decision he was struggling with, he didn't go to those girls who flirted with him—the girls who hugged him tightly, sat in his lap, or acted like big teases.

He opened up to me because I was his friend. I'd chosen to be genuine with him. Sure, we joked around but never crossed that unspoken line. Eric and I were in homeroom together for four years. I never got to pucker up and touch my lips to his. I never got to squeeze his big biceps or run my fingers through that blond hair. But I got to do something more important—I got to touch his heart!

Flirting can be fun. But it makes a girl seem insincere, cotton candyish, easy to acquire.

Proverbs 31:30 says that "charm is deceitful" (NASB). That puts it plain and simple.

Will you choose to be the real deal? Will you choose to be a flirt or a friend? Would you rather have a flirty five-day romance or a lasting friendship? The choice is yours.

B.A.B.E.s, there needs to be a clear difference in us because of our connection to Christ.

Are You a Tease?

Take this test to find out how you score on the B.A.B.E. tease-o-meter! Circle the letter that best describes you.

1. Your friends say your eyes are . . .
   A. friendly
   B. honest
   C. sexy

2. You prefer . . .
   A. Cover Girl cosmetics
   B. Mary Kay cosmetics
   C. M.A.C. cosmetics

3. Your style is . . .
   A. athletic
   B. all-American doll
   C. ElleGirl lookalike

4. When might you show cleavage (or try to!)?
   A. in a swim team suit
   B. never
   C. when you wear a low-cut top

5. It's most important for you to be . . .
   A. happy
   B. yourself
   C. accepted

6. It's chilly, and you're going to a football game. Which jacket would you wear?
   A. a denim jacket over a hoodie
   B. the scarf your grandma made with a slim-cut jacket
   C. forget the jacket!— you'd wear a satin top with lace trim (you don't get cold)

7. When sitting on the floor, you . . .
   A. hunch forward
   B. sit up straight
   C. lean back on both hands

8. When you choose your outfit, you . . .
   A. think about what will be most comfortable
   B. think about looking modest but still cool
   C. think about how to catch a certain guy's eye

9. When you're on the gym floor, you . . .
   A. keep your legs together
   B. cross them at the knee/ankle
   C. sit Indian style or with ankles three feet apart

10. When that cute guy struts into biology lab, you . . .
    A. barely notice
    B. sit up a bit straighter
    C. run your fingers through your hair and whip out your lip gloss

Count up the number of As, then multiply that number by 10. Count your Bs, then multiply that number by 20. Do the same with the Cs, then multiply by 30.

As_____ Bs_____ Cs _____

Add up your scores for As, Bs, and Cs, and mark your total score on the tease-o-meter below.

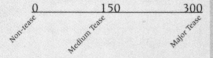

Are you pleased with the results? Do you need to make some changes? Are there guys who are misinterpreting your actions? Do you wonder why some guys seem to come on to you?

Lots of girls tease guys for fun. They want to see if they can make a guy notice them or make him want them. But the fun ends when a guy interprets the teasing as an invitation to pursue the girl sexually. So be aware. What do your eyes say? What does your body communicate? Are your clothes sending the message of your heart? What are your actions expressing? Think it through; talk it over with a friend.

How to Ruin a Good Guy-Girl Friendship in Five Easy Steps

Step 1: Sit super close.
Step 2: Hold hands.
Step 3: Kiss.
Step 4: Fondle and caress.
Step 5: Have sex.

Follow these five steps to botch up your friendship with a guy. Sexual stuff changes relationships. It turns time you used to spend studying, grabbing a burger, or gathering a group for Ultimate Frisbee into time spent looking for places to be alone and make out. And no, once your relationship crosses the line, you really can't ever again just be friends. ●

"If you really are just friends, stay in public places when you do things together."
Greg, 15

"Guys are visually turned on. . . . He may very well think that if you're willing to bare it, you're willing to share it. Remember that there's a difference between like and lust. . . . Dress with class and you'll be treated with a higher standard of respect. . . . It's that simple."* Tammy Bennett

"Having friendships with girls has been great. I didn't grow up with sisters, so I really didn't know how to act or talk to girls or relate to them. I've learned so much about what they like and don't like, and hey, I can even read their emotions sometimes!"
Mark, 17

*Check out this quote in Tammy's book *Guys, Dating, and Sex* (Grand Rapids: Revell, 2005), 65.

Coed Craziness

Lighten up and enjoy guys as friends. Here are more ideas for mixing it up.

Freaky Facts! Plan to meet at the local library, a used book store, or a Barnes and Noble. Give everyone thirty minutes to find the weirdest book with bizarre information. Meet at a specific location and page through the books, sharing the freakiest facts with your friends. Then put the books back (yep, in the right places) and go grab a latte or peppermint mocha.

Team It Up! Organize a team sport like softball or Ultimate Frisbee. Choose a time, date, and location and let everyone know. (This is the perfect opportunity to be inclusive, not exclusive. Tell everyone to invite two or three other teens.) Have a few friends help you gather up whatever's needed for the sport you select. Be there early so new people won't be wandering around alone feeling like the butt of a practical joke! Divide into teams in a nonthreatening way, meaning don't have two team captains pick their teams. Instead, try this. Bring several packs of two different flavors of individually wrapped bubble gum—let's say watermelon and blue raspberry. If you have twenty teens, have ten of one flavor and ten of the other. Now randomly toss the gum and tell everyone to catch a piece. Then announce, "Team one is the watermelons, and team two is the blue raspberries." Now get playing . . . batter up! Other options: flag football, basketball, capture the flag, soccer, badminton, bowling, or even hockey!

Eating Backward! Instead of having a progressive dinner, throw it in reverse and have a "regressive" dinner! Start with dessert (who won't like that?), then serve the main meal (entrée), followed by the salad and the soup, and top it all off with appetizers! So let's say you're having Italian cuisine. Serve tiramisu or cheesecake, then lasagna, garlic bread, antipasto salad, minestrone soup, then mini pizza rolls. Be creative with your menu. If you want to take it further, choose invitations, table decorations, napkin folds, and decorations to go with the theme of your dinner. (A theme can be based on the style of food being served—in this case Italian—a holiday, or the reason for the party—birthday, last day of school, driver's license celebration, or whatever!)

If you and your friends don't want to undertake the whole cooking thing, do your regressive dinner fast-food style. The food is eaten in the same backward order, just go to a different fast-food restaurant for each item. Note: check out who offers the best dessert options first!

God designed guys to develop into leaders, protectors, providers—so let a guy help fix your bike chain, download your fav tunes onto your IPod, carry your fifty-pound backpack, and open the door for you. Doing things for you (even things you could do for yourself) comes naturally to most guys. Admittedly, these traits will be seen in some guys much later than in others—it's a part of maturing into a godly gentleman. These things don't make a guy weak, and it doesn't mean he's falling for you. Let him play his God-given role.

THE GREAT DATE WAIT

THE BACHELORETTE

She's never the forlorn daughter of a pig farmer in mid-America. Instead, she's a well-educated, petite bombshell with highlights and heels. And we're supposed to believe she can't land a man! Who coined the term *reality TV*, anyway?

The Bachelorette has a basic strategy. Lasso up about fifteen lover boys; force them to shave, shower, and slap on cologne; dress them in penguin suits; then parade them around the maiden with the ringless third finger of her left hand. Then one by one she interviews, scrutinizes, flirts, and even goes so far as to sleep with a few (in the olden days, the prince simply had to kiss Snow White to be the winner). Now it's time to eliminate. She must decide if she prefers Tony's keen sense of humor to Nick's sensitive nature. Or maybe Steffan the stockbroker with his love for the outdoors would be the perfect match for her.

Plucking them one at a time as if from a garden of guys, she narrows her options to two (by now all the women in America have placed their bets and have their eyes glued to the box). At this point, she gets to take them each home to meet the family, who can then discuss the guy's pros and cons. Who best meets her criteria? Who's funny, tall, insightful, crazy about dogs, honest, and romantic? Who enhances her personality, letting her be her best self? Who can provide a solid financial future? After a long, sleepless night, she finally makes her decision. Whew!

B.A.B.E.s, this is *not* the way God works.

He isn't going to parade a bunch of guys in front of you and let you take them on a test drive to decide who's your ultimate dreamboat.

Likewise, you don't have to dive into the dating pool to find a guy who will rescue you from drowning in the pressure to be going out with someone. You don't have to fret over ever finding someone who perfectly fits your list of must-haves.

I'm not implying that you can't take note of the characteristics or qualities you hope to have in your hunk-o-hubby, but beware of making a list, searching out a guy who matches your criteria, then declaring him God's choice for you. No, that would be *your* choice for you. I've heard girls say things like, "I'm definitely marrying a guy with blue eyes, because I want my kids to have blue eyes," "My husband has to be a patient guy, since I'm so impatient," "There's no way I would go to a Pentecostal church, so my man can't be one of those," "I absolutely want my guy to work out with me—I adore biceps," and "I would be miserable with a guy who's unromantic."

Don't put God in a box. Let him surprise you. Remember, he knows you inside and out, loves you more than anyone else possibly could, and will give you what's best for you. Realistically, being human, you can't be fully aware of what's best for you. You can't see the future. Your heavenly Father can.

So how does God work when it comes to the guy thing? Let's go back to the very beginning. Adam was hanging out with the animals, getting bored and lonely. So God knocked him out, swiped one of his ribs, then formed his final creation (his majestic masterpiece, if you ask me). He included the exact combination of characteristics that would create the woman who would fulfill, delight, and challenge Adam. (In almost every way, she was his exact opposite! We chatted about this earlier in the book.) Then God placed Eve at the far end of the garden, telling her to stay under bushes, sneak behind waterfalls, or shimmy up trees—anything to keep Adam from finding her! God was going to get a huge kick out of watching the world's first game of hide-and-seek!

Are you scratching your head thinking, *What? I don't remember reading that part of the story.* That's because that's *not* what happened. See for yourself.

> So the LORD God caused the man to fall into a deep sleep; and while he was sleeping, he took one of the man's ribs and closed up the place with flesh. Then the LORD God made a woman from the rib he had taken out of the man, and **he brought her to the man.**
>
> Genesis 2:21–22 NIV

God did what? He took Eve by the hand and led her straight to Adam. He brought her—personally escorted her—to the man he had ready and waiting. He did the same with Isaac and Rebecca, Ruth and Boaz, and many others). And he can do the same for you.

Now close the book and think about this for a bit. Then refill your glass of water (you need eight a day) and get back here. We have a few more things to discuss!

God didn't initiate the relationships between Sampson and Delilah or David and Bathsheba. They ended up being messy, painful, and life altering. Wait for your mate!

Who's in Charge of Your Love Life?

Sonia withdrew the steaming latte from her lips and shook her head. Looking at me with the saddest eyes, she said, "I was so stupid. My school friends all date, and I couldn't stand being called 'lesbo' or 'frigid' just because I didn't have a boyfriend. Plus, my mom kept suggesting dateable guys to me, like she's embarrassed that her daughter isn't getting the guys. So I caved. And now I can't take it back or erase it."

Who's in control of your love life? Are you letting others influence you in a negative way? Or are you the girl who tries to date anything wearing boxers? Either way, you might be making the wrong choices. Here's my advice:

Leave your love life up to the Lord!

Whew! Did that just bite you like a fire ant? Let's define a few things here—always a bonus for searching out deeper meanings.

leave: put it down; don't touch it; go forward without it; submit it to someone else's control

love life: romantic relationships; starry-eyed endeavors; affectionate attachments

up to: to the choice of; to the discretion of; to the decision of

the Lord: the One who rules over everything (sovereign), the One you (hopefully) serve and obey out of love; the One who calls the shots; the One who can be trusted because he knows your heart, your needs, and your future

I'm going to pull all this together for you and hit you with a challenge. Are you up for it? Here goes.

Because the Lord is sovereign, loving, and able, are you willing to trust him to bring the right guy into your life at the right time?

Roll it over in your brain as long as you need, then write your answer here: _____
_____
_____
_____
_____
_____

If you doubt, check yourself. Are you questioning something about the Lord God—does he really care, is he truly in control, or what? Do you doubt yourself? Are you afraid to totally trust him? Do you think you know best? These are issues you need to settle in your heart of hearts! They'll affect the way you respond to the stuff life throws at you.

Here are four things I know will help you.

First, get a copy of *Bible B.A.B.E.s: The Inside Dish on Divine Divas.* You'll read about how God arranged the circumstances for Esther to become queen and save the Jews from slaughter. You'll discover that God knew the perfect time to answer Hannah's prayer to have a baby, *and* he had a plan for that child to become a priest, a judge, and a prophet. You'll be amazed at the way he loved and forgave Eve in spite of her blatant disobedience. Then there's Bathsheba—she shows why God is worth trusting even in the most painful circumstances. And those are only a few examples. Real-life story after real-life story (you do understand that the Bible is true and that these B.A.B.E.s really existed, right?) will serve as witness to the Lord's faithful handiwork in the lives of teen girls and women who trusted him as Lord. He *is* trustworthy!

Second, do word studies on *trust, Lord, sovereign, love,* and *surrender.* Take each word and define it from the dictionary, thesaurus (gives synonyms/similar words and antonyms/opposite words), and a Bible concordance (directs you to Scriptures that use that word). Pray over what you've discovered. Then, in your own words, write a fresh definition of each word you studied.

Third, arrange to meet with your youth director, your pastor, your Bible study leader, a parent, an aunt—any adult in your life who knows a lot about the Bible. Don't just gather up a bunch of opinions. Get Bible facts. Why adults? They have more experiences than your friends and have journeyed through life with Jesus longer. So pull the plug on your questions and concerns. Adults *love* answering questions for teenagers. I see it all the time.

Fourth, ask the Lord to show you personally that he's trustworthy (not that he *ever* has to prove anything to you or me or anyone). But if you ask, you need to pay attention and not just chalk his answer up to coincidence. If you've seriously prayed, it will be God.

So if you take the babe-a-liciously bold step of trusting the Lord to bring the right person—*his* guy for you—into your life when *he* knows it's best, what are you to do in the meantime? You rock in the question category. I'll attempt to answer. But first, take a glance at Lisa's story. ●

My Virgin Lips:
Why I'm Glad I'm Still Saving My First Kiss
by Lisa Velthouse

A few years ago, if the subject of first kisses came up in conversation, my lips were sealed completely. Even in the company of my best friends and family, I wouldn't talk about first kisses if my life depended on it. Why? Because back then just the idea of stating the real facts seemed humiliating. I was insecure to the core about what I would have to admit.

Here's the honest-to-goodness truth: without really intending to, I managed to make it all the way through middle school, high school, and college without ever being given a single smooch. That's right; I got a college diploma before I got just one little kiss (or asked out on a single date!).

Believe me, I never thought I would be that girl, the one who was continually *not* in a dating relationship. When I was growing up, I daydreamed about candlelight dinners and strolls along the beach and all that typical "he loves me, he loves me not" stuff. In math class, I doodled my signature to see what it would look like if it ended with the last name of that cute guy at the next desk. I was forever playing the role of the starry-eyed romantic, so (okay, I confess) it was a total shock to me that guys weren't banging down my door.

It's not that I thought I was super special or anything like that. Really. I simply thought that most (like 96 percent) of all high school and college girls dated, not to mention got kissed. So since I was clearly one of the 4 percent of dateless/kissless gals out there, I figured there was something dreadfully wrong with me. I was convinced that there must be one (or many!) reasons why guys weren't asking me out. *Maybe I'm ugly*, I thought, *or annoying, too confident, not stylish enough, not funny enough, not thin enough.* You name it.

But as the story goes, I grew up. Over time I started seeing things differently. Really, really differently.

You know what's great about a life like this? You don't regret the kisses you gave away too hastily. Your heart doesn't have to heal, because it's never been broken. You don't feel bad because you almost went too far on prom night. You get the chance to discover who you are before you wind up in a relationship. You can look ahead without ever having to look back first. You have more time to grow closer to God and to focus on experiencing his love. Trust me, the list goes on and on. It's spectacular.

And speaking of reality, my romance-free high school and college years had very little to do with my looks, my personality, my style, my humor, or my weight. Let's face it: if I had wanted a date badly enough, I could've gotten one. Any day, a girl can put on a miniskirt and a tube top, walk into a party, and get *that* kind of attention. If she's willing to cheapen herself enough, she can get all the dates and kisses she wants. But they'd be cheapened dates and cheapened kisses. I want—I *deserve*—more than that.

So these days, when the topic surfaces, I go ahead and tell people the truth, and I don't hesitate. I'm twenty-three years old, and I've (still) never been kissed! I'm not embarrassed about my virgin lips anymore; in fact, I'm thrilled to tell other girls about them. On a regular basis, I meet girls who are just like I used to be: embarrassed and insecure about their lack of romance and dreaming that one day life will be fabulous. But they still think it takes dates and kisses for life to be that good.

Somebody's gotta tell those girls they're missing out, and that's why I'm so thankful I can tell my story. Although twenty-three-and-never-been-kissed wasn't ever something I hoped for, I wouldn't trade it for anything. After all, who *wouldn't* want to be this happy? I've written my first book (*Saving My First Kiss*), and I have a great job, great girlfriends, time for family, time to be a youth leader, even time to travel and be a speaker on The B.A.B.E. Seminar™ tour! I'm smitten with the life I've got, and I'm smiling all the way from my toes. I've learned the truth about never-been-kissed, and I get to share it—and that's always a lip-smacking good time.

Lisa Velthouse is a tall, redheaded B.A.B.E. who was selected as 2000 *Brio* Girl. She's continually amazed at God's eternally significant plan for her life. Get to know her better at www.lisavelthouse.com!

Kisses are like diamonds . . . the more of them there are in circulation, the less valuable they are.

Benefits of Being Single

You can totally be yourself without worrying if a guy is impressed or embarrassed.

You can watch a bunch of chick flicks while eating popcorn by the handful.

You never have to stress over having a fight with your boyfriend that could ruin your whole day.

You never have to think about having kissable breath.

You can make fun and wacky weekend plans with your girlfriends.

You don't risk being pressured into becoming sexually involved.

You never have to worry about what you would do if you got pregnant.

You won't get into the harmful pattern of dating, breaking up, dating, breaking up, and so on.

You can focus your time and energy on developing your God-given gifts and special abilities. (To discover what those might be, go to www.andreastephens.com to take a cool spiritual gifts quiz.)

"I believe that the same God who keeps the earth spinning and gravity pulling can bring the right two people together at the right time and in the right place. We should just pay attention to his hand at work as we go about our daily stuff and not get sucked into seeking after the perfect relationship. Besides, if we really want his will in our lives, we need to do things his way." Gregory, 18

WHILE YOU WAIT TO DATE

When you choose to trust God with your love life, you can quit worrying about your dating status and your love quota. Going the *wait-to-date* route is cool. It gives you time and energy to put elsewhere. Yep, delaying your dating career until after high school (or longer) sets you free to pursue other interests, other aspects of life. Here are some tips on things to do *in the meantime*!

- Be about the Father's business. Paul (no, not the Boylander in your chemistry class, the Bible dude who wrote most of the New Testament) wished everyone would be single like he was so they could focus on God's work instead of being wrapped up in that lovin' feeling, trying to please the object of their affection (1 Corinthians 7:34). There's something God wants you to be doing right now. Pray about what it is, then get after it, B.A.B.E.!

- Hang out at youth group and church. Jesus was only twelve when he got so wrapped up talking with the guys in the temple that he missed the caravan home! When his frantic parents finally found him, he was like, "Stop freaking. Where else did you expect me to be? I'm just chillin' at church!" Actually, "'Why were you searching for me?' he asked. 'Didn't you know I had to be in my Father's house?'" (Luke 2:49 NIV). Some girls drop church to be alone with their guy. Big mistake. You be the wise one who stays tight with her church friends.

"Most teenagers my age are really into dating, but not me. Why? Well, I prefer not to. You see, society places strong pressures on teens to date—through the media, entertainment industry, and such—and this leads to many shallow relationships that deflate your true value as a person. Since I have decided not to date, I am able to build more healthy relationships with guys and have fun friendships with them without getting too serious. This allows me to 'study and analyze' different attitudes and personalities. Without the responsibility and the dedication that a dating relationships requires, I can be completely focused on God and his plan for my life. I can build character and develop into the woman God designed me to be before sharing my heart with another person. Dating requires maturity, responsibility, and character. It is better to do it founded on strong, solid bases and in the right time than on premature bases as a delicate experiment that plays with the heart. The important thing is to trust God and his timing and to not feel pressured by the doubting thought of 'Am I ever going to find someone?' I am sure that God is preparing that man for me just as he is preparing me!" Susana Gutierrez Moreno, 17, *Brio* Girl top four finalist, 2006

- Study the handbook to life! That would be the Bible! What you learn about God, Jesus, spiritual principles, and the lives of others who have loved and served God will impact your life in a way nothing else can. Get in a Bible study or start one. Make your teen years all about God!

- Set your affections on things above rather than on the boy next door! What things matter to Jesus? What's valuable in the kingdom of God? Let these types of things have top priority in your heart (Matthew 6:21; Colossians 3:2).

- Get tight with your girlfriends. Some of these B.A.B.E.s are going to be around the rest of your life. Some will be in your wedding. Some will walk with you through the tough times to come. These are relationships worth investing in.

- Take a class offered through your local parks and recreation department. What have you always wanted to try? Karate? Cake decorating? Computer programming? Ballroom dancing (this is very fun to do with some friends)? Go for it.

- Sign up for a college class—on campus or online. Gaining knowledge can make you a well-rounded, interesting B.A.B.E.! Then using that knowledge makes you wise. Besides, the more you know, the more you know!

- Say yes to those extra babysitting or odd jobs and save your big bucks for something cool like the *Brio* magazine mission trip! Grab the lowdown at www.briomag.com/missions. Teen Mania offers some awesome trips too. Check it out at www.teenmania.com! I believe every teen should be involved with missions. God uses missions to teach you things and touch your heart in ways that don't happen at home when you're easily distracted (well, like some of us are). Be of good courage and go for it!

- You'll avoid the date-breakup-date-breakup pattern. Few people marry a guy they dated in junior high or high school. So a girl dates someone for a while. Then it ends. Breakup. Hot guy asks her out. Then she realizes he's all hot air! Breakup.

On and on. Then one day she walks down the aisle pledging forever love to her groom. But when they hit a bunch of really rough spots, she does what she's been doing all her life . . . breakup. Can it be that all the dating and breaking up sets people up for divorce? God asks us to stay married forever. This is one reason you need to know that you know that you know you're marrying God's guy for you. Then when it gets tough (and all marriages get tough), you'll work through it instead of bolting.

- Do the group thing! Spend time with guys in group settings. This helps you get to know them without the pressure of single dating or potential romance. Guys are totally fun to be around (most of the time), and this is the perfect way to do it. Plus, it's way more fun to be with more people.

- Pray for your hunk-o-hubby now! Your guy is alive this very second. God knows who he is, where he lives, and what he's doing. Start praying for him. Include stuff like devotion to Christ, development of integrity, faithfulness to his commitments, sexual purity, honoring his parents, and studies. Ask the Lord to prepare your hearts for each other.

- Stay focused on the greater purpose of your teen years! This is the time of life to develop your personality, your gifts, your talents, your hobbies, your interests, and your future. Dating can quickly throw a girl off course and steal precious time. Refocus your God-given abilities and purpose!

No doubt if you wait to single date, people will be nosy, wanting to know why. Go ahead and explain and then tack on a lighthearted comment about some famous hot guy like, "I'm holding out for _____" or "I'm waiting for _____ to discover I'm alive" or "I'm secretly engaged to _____."

"Father, you sent the stars, like leftover sand you scattered through the universe, to cover me like a wild embrace. You sent a soft breeze to push the hair out of my face, to leave me breathless and excited. It was the most romantic moment of my life. And its all ours—just yours and mine." Natalie

Pure Love

Pure love. It's about moonlit nights, picnics by candlelight, and surprise presents. It's about two bodies in the passion of the moment, merging into one. Wait. Is this really what pure love is about? Look into the Bible's famous love chapter.

> Love is patient and kind. Love is not jealous or boastful or proud or rude. Love does not demand its own way. Love is not irritable, and it keeps no record of when it has been wronged. It is never glad about injustice but rejoices whenever the truth wins out. Love never gives up, never loses faith, is always hopeful, and endures through every circumstance. Love will last forever.
>
> 1 Corinthians 13:4–8 NLT

Pure love is about action. Describe what it looks like: _____

_____

_____

_____

Pure love is about attitudes. List them here: ____

_____

_____

"When girls stare at me, I don't know if it's because they think I'm cute or gross." Mark, 14

Pure love is about forever. Describe what you think that will feel like: _____

_____

_____

Pure love is the type of love God has for you and the type of love he desires for you to be given by the guy he brings into your life in the future. ●

Feeling attractive is more about your God-Confidence and God-Beauty than about being arm in arm with a guy. If you don't feel pretty, you're the only one who can change it.

"I would rather be known for my personality and character than anything physical. I want a girl to want to be around me because of who I am rather than how I look or what kind of car I drive or whatever. I'm a guy with substance, and I believe God will lead me to the same type of girl." Scott, 17

Love Letter—From the Heart of a Dad

Darling Katie,

You are my pride and joy! I never imagined what kind of impact you would have on my life or how deeply I would be able to love someone. It is because of this love that I write this note to you. I know you have interests in your life other than soccer, singing, and the like. Boys are looming on the horizon. Therefore, here's a list of some things to think about as you reach the age for girl-guy relationships.

Put God first! Above all else, put God first in every aspect of your life—especially when it comes to guys. He is the one who has your best interest at heart, and he will provide direction. Talk to him. Search him out. Ask him anything. He has promised you much—take him up on it.

Boys—Bad! All right, not really—at least not all of them. I'm sure there are a lot of nice guys out there. Choose someone who will respect you as a person and also respect your wishes. He'll be the guy who cares more about you than he does about himself. He won't try to change you—he'll love who you are. He'll be patient, kind, caring, loving, and thoughtful, and he will rejoice at those qualities in you.

Communicate with us. Keep a dialog open with your mom and me. Believe it or not, we were young once, and we even dated a little bit way back then. We have some pretty good experience in this area—use it!

Value friendships over romantic relationships. The most successful relationships—those that last a lifetime—are usually born from a wonderful, solid friendship. Where boys are concerned—go slow. Get to know who they really are—what they truly believe and how they support you through both good and bad times. There can be friendship without romance, but no romance can last without friendship.

Be yourself. You don't have to jump into the guy-girl thing just because your friends have. It's a decision you and God should make together—keep it that way. Surround yourself with friends who have your best interests at heart. You'll know who they are.

Don't choose a guy just because Mom and I like him. I can't believe I even wrote that. Dig in and try to understand this one. Even though we may claim to know everything, we may not. Only God knows the innermost longings of your heart. Just because Mom and Dad like a guy doesn't necessarily mean he's the right guy for you. It is still your call, and I'm confident you'll choose wisely. Bottom line, always lean on the Holy Spirit.

Communicate with us. This deserves to be in here twice. I know you are a great communicator, and for that I am most grateful! I am praying that this communication will continue and grow as you also grow. Please know that we are a team and you can come to us with anything.

I hope you also know what a true joy you are to me. It is because of you my life has meaning. You are truly a gift from God, and the sun shines when you are close by!

With never-ending love,
Dad

WHEN YOU'RE NOT THE ONE!

Even if you've made the decision to delay dating, you can't always stop your natural attraction to a fine specimen of the male species. Your heart jumps, your pulse quickens, your mouth does the slow drop, and your stud-muffin radar locks in on him. When that drip of drool splashes onto your arm, you're quickly brought back to the moment. Without fair warning, you find yourself in the center of a full-blown crush.

Then you remember. You're not looking for a boyfriend. But your interest in exploring a friendship takes flight. Too much flight. It soars. But the interest isn't mutual. Here's what happened with Erin.

Erin tried hard to keep her secret, but she feared that the fact that she was totally taken with Marc was beginning to show. Just yesterday when he greeted her on his way into the library, she felt her cheeks turn ten shades of red while her heart launched into orbit. Surely the whole school had noticed.

But would Marc notice tonight at the basketball game? Erin overheard him tell his friends he'd be there. So would she. Nothing could keep her away. After all, she'd spent the last three weeks nonchalantly showing up wherever Marc showed up. He was always friendly, and she hoped he was starting to like her enough to spark real conversation. Maybe tonight would be the night that she could really get to know him. Maybe tonight she would actually sit near him or even *with* him.

Erin spent an hour in pregame prep. She went through her mental checklist. Hair—straight and smooth. Lip gloss—shiny. Breath—fresh. Outfit—to die for! She even practiced flashing a few smiles into the mirror before she headed out to the game with her friend Sara.

Once inside the gym, her scan began. She quickly spotted him. Bleachers, left side, top row. Whoa! She instantly noticed that the emerald sweatshirt really complemented his blond hair and gorgeous smile as he casually laughed and joked with his buddies and with . . . *Wait!*

A wave of panic clutched her throat.

Who was *that*?

Who was that girl who just scooched closer to him, the girl he just put his arm around?

Doing what any logical girl would do, she sent Sara to snoop around and find out. The news wasn't good. A girlfriend? Marc had a *girlfriend*? Someone from the high school across town? For real?

Her heart and her hopes raced to see which one would hit bottom first.

Reality set in. Marc had a special friend, all right. In fact, *more* than a friend, and it was *not* her!

Ever been in Erin's shoes or in a similar pair? Ever wanted to develop a friendship with someone who wasn't interested in getting to know you? Maybe you *did* get to know the guy only to be ignored a few months later. Maybe the guy didn't like you when he realized you weren't his typical party-girl type. Maybe your parents refused to let you hang out with the guy because they could see the stars in your eyes and knew your motives were a bit mixed up!

Whatever the scenario, the truth that **you are not the one** can threaten to land a girl on her tush! Not a fun place to be!

Here are some don'ts and dos for handling those unwelcome feelings of rejection. They'll get you back up on your feet—fast!

Whether a guy wants to be your friend or not, you are worth it!

Don'ts!

- **Don't forget your first love!** That's Jesus! When you set your sights too heavily on anyone but him, you set yourself up for a big fall. Jesus will never break your heart!
- **Don't drop your guard!** Protect your heart from the temptation to be shot with Cupid's arrow. Keep friendship as your goal.
- **Don't let your emotions take over!** Feelings are fickle, and they can steer you in the wrong direction, thus causing you to draw the wrong conclusions about yourself or your situation. When you feel upset, go release those emotions with a good hard cry or a good hard workout. Feelings aside, you can get a fresh perspective.
- **Don't lose your self-esteem!** Ninety-nine percent of girls who get rejected respond by questioning themselves. *Am I not good enough, cute enough, thin enough, smart enough, rich enough, hip enough? How can I be what he wants*? Stop it! This would be a good time to record all the special things about yourself and

all the blessings you have in your life! Focus on those! Don't let rejection rock your confidence.

- **Don't devalue yourself!** Beware! So many girls think they're less valuable without a certain guy's approval. *Big lie!* Your value as a person isn't based on your popularity or dating status. It's based on God. As Christians, we've been purchased by the Most High God who paid the incredibly high price of his own Son just to have us as his own! You are very valuable!

Dos!

- **Do acknowledge the pain!** Of course it hurts to be shut out and rejected. You don't have to put on a brave front and deny it. Let it out. Write it out. Talk it out. Cry out to the Lord. Psalm 34:18 tells us, "The Lord is close to the brokenhearted and saves those who are crushed in spirit" (NIV). Do remember, not everyone we want to be friends with will want to be friends with us. It's just a fact of life.

- **Do keep God as the center of your life!** In the Psalms, David refers to God as his solid rock. When you build your life on the Rock, you won't be shaken quite so hard when people come and go. Let's face it—friends are fickle, and guys can be jerks. With God as your center, your life will remain intact no matter what hurricane threatens to blow you over! God's friendship is unchanging.

- **Do control your self-talk!** If you keep playing the scene or conversation over and over in your mind, it can cause you to spiral downward into depression. Challenge yourself to think and say positive things *to* yourself.

- **Do celebrate *you*!** Yep, treat yourself to a Chunky Monkey sundae or a hot new pair of shoes while you take note of all your special qualities and God-given traits. Celebrate who you are in Christ and who you're becoming as a B.A.B.E. who seeks to serve and please your heavenly Father.

Coed Craziness

Okay, you know the drill! Get up off the couch, phone a friend, poll the group, and throw out the lifelines! Have a blast building friendships with the opposite sex. Remember, group activities allow you to watch and learn and to *interact, not attract!*

Pizza Pie Construction! Yep, you can pull in some doughy facts about your friends while building pizzas. Here's the deal. Let everyone know the who, what, where, and when. Assign each person an item to bring. Here's the catch—don't tell them what you're going to do with the item they bring. So call Susie Q. and ask her to bring a fresh veggie that's green (like broccoli). Someone else brings a veggie that's red (like tomatoes or red peppers) or yellow (like squash or corn) or orange (like carrots). Have others bring cheeses—yellow, white, spicy. Can't forget the meat! Assign these by the animal! Gather meat from a cow, a pig, or a chicken (BBQ chicken pizza is scrumptious). Throw in a few sauces—alfredo, BBQ, taco—and you provide the pizza sauce and the crust so they can't guess what's up. As they arrive, spread the ingredients out so they can see their choices. Some ingredients will require cutting or chopping. Put two or three people on one pizza crust (or you could offer small crusts for individual pizzas or give some guys their own regular-size pizzas). Now turn them loose to construct a masterpiece pizza! While you're eating, challenge them to construct a devotional message around Paul's teaching in 1 Corinthians 12:12–27. How can the cheese say to the crust, "I don't need you?" . . .

A Night at the Improv! Find out who's a true extrovert. Catch some clues on how to do improv from reruns of *Whose Line Is It Anyway?* Write a phrase like "sports fan" or "old man retrieving something from a street drain" or "Peter trying to get the five thousand hungry people to sit down to be fed—include his reaction to the twelve baskets left over" or any situation that can be acted out. You can use ideas from a charades game if you get stuck, or open the Gospels to check out the parables. Designate a specific area to be the stage. If it's elevated and has lights directed toward it, great. Call for the first volunteer. Let him (or her) select a folded piece of paper with the situation written on it; then watch him react when he opens it up to see what he has to act out. That's half the fun. Now invite him to take the stage, and let the improv begin. Serving popcorn and sodas is a must for this one.

People Watching! This isn't nearly as dull as it may sound. Gather at a busy place like an indoor or outdoor mall, a marketplace area, a coffee shop, outside the theater on a Saturday, or wherever. Really be observant as you watch people. Now tell their stories. Where are they from? How old are they? What are their occupations? What types of cars do they drive? What are they shopping for? (or what movie are they seeing?) Where are they headed? Where do they get their hair cut? On and on. Make up the pieces as you put each person's whole story together. If your group has their creative juices flowing, this can be a kick. When you're all laughed out, go grab a taco.

Kindness Day! Show the guys that being a B.A.B.E. in Action is all about doing stuff for others—kind stuff. So declare an official Random Acts of Kindness Day. Do some preplanning but be willing to scrap the plans if the Lord leads you to a few different kindnesses once you get rolling. Here are some action ideas: Buy a few bouquets of flowers (grocery store or flower shop) and split them up so you can go pass out flowers one by one to people in a nursing home or retirement center. Don't assume the elderly gentlemen won't want a flower—some of them may have loved gardening in their younger days. You can rake leaves; mow a yard; wash windows; babysit; surprise someone with a home-cooked dinner; bake cookies and give them out; write anonymous notes to your teachers, coaches, tutors, or anyone you want to encourage. Tell them what you appreciate or admire about them.

"Most of the people I've been around are single but are constantly searching for a way to get hooked up. Until a few years ago, I wanted a boyfriend just as much as the next girl. Then I made a huge discovery. Being single is a gift! These are precious years from God, a phase when you have all the time in the world to give your heart to him and create a beautiful love story with God. It's wise to learn to value every season of your life, including singleness." Rachel, 17

Expert Advice from Single B.A.B.E. Know-It-All Michelle McKinney Hammond

"The Bible is the longest and best love letter ever written! Instead of just reading the Bible as a reference book or as a how-to guide on Christianity, read it as if you were reading God's private journal. Ask God to guide you to the specific Scriptures that reveal his heart toward you. Begin to journal the things that he shares with you, and then write him back in the form of a love letter. If people can fall in love over the Internet, falling in love with God should be a cinch!

"We step into *real intimacy* with the Lord by worshipping him in spirit and in truth—now that's true intimacy. In fact, *praise and worship are the deepest forms of intimacy* you can experience with Christ. When you truly press past yourself and into the Holy of Holies within your spirit, opening your hands and confessing that they are empty. Extending your arms and proclaiming them helpless without him; submitting your body to be a vessel used only for the Master's purposes. The more you do it, the more you will want to do it. He is the 'lover of our souls' and we feel it when we worship."*

If you're trying to get a guy to like you, check yourself. Are you purposely showing up everywhere he goes? Have you changed the way you dress, hoping he'll notice your figure and savvy fashion sense? Are you texting him several times a day?

If you answered yes to any of these questions, you're probably being fake, manipulative, and deceptive and are afraid he won't like you for who you really are. This shows you're not ready to date. Only when you can be yourself can a friendship, then a relationship, flourish. ●

"Loyalty makes a person attractive." Proverbs 19:22 NLT

*Find this quote and more of Michelle's advice in her book *Get a Love Life*! Don't stop there. Discover more about this author, speaker, producer, and singing B.A.B.E. at www.michellemckinneyhammond.com.

Life as a B.A.B.E. in
BOYLAND

It's been quite a journey, this trip you and I have taken together through Boyland. I hope that at this point you'll agree—guys aren't as weird or mysterious as they used to be. God did a pretty great thing when he designed the male gender—testosterone and all! This is a good thing, since life on planet earth will always involve guys in some way, shape, or form.

When you've caught the B.A.B.E. wave, surfing life with confidence in who you are as a young woman who is beautiful, accepted, blessed, and eternally significant, it will be evident. You won't be tossed around in the tidal wave of the world's teachings on guys, sex, love, beauty, and so on. You know the truth about these issues based on the Bible.

And you know who will notice?

Boylanders!

They'll notice that you have God-Beauty that shines as you focus on others.

They'll notice that you aren't fighting for their attention—you have an awesome audience of One.

They'll notice that you're comfortable in your own skin and choose to dress in comfort and with modesty.

They'll notice that you're pursuing your *holy* passions, wanting to be the kind of B.A.B.E. God can use for significant assignments.

They'll notice that you've made a commitment to sexual (and mental) purity and abstinence.

They'll notice that *you* like *you* and don't need a boyfriend to feel good about yourself.

They'll notice that you're not hanging out with nothing to do—you're way into taking keyboard lessons, getting ready for soccer camp, or leading the games for VBS. You're developing your special abilities and spiritual gifts.

They'll notice your desire to be a faithful friend, a loving daughter, a good student.

They'll notice your inclusive, energetic spirit, because you're always pulling together a group of girls and guys for some good, wholesome fun.

They'll notice your effort to ask questions to genuinely get to know who they are on the inside.

They'll notice that you accept them as they are.

They'll notice . . . you. And it will be for all the right reasons.

Ah. You're such a B.A.B.E.! And personally, I'm proud of you!

●

Life in Boyland will be an enriching experience.

B.A.B.E.S aND BOYS IN ACTION!

Get it together—a group of guys and girls, that is! Spending time with a mix of your guy and girl friends can give you a greater glimpse into the mysterious ways of the male gender. It lets you see them just being themselves! See how they interact and how you interact with them.

By now you've noticed the Coed Craziness sections, right? I've included them to give you suggestions on things to do in group settings. Perhaps something you read generated a cool idea of your own. Great.

I have included, and would suggest, three types of activities.

First, there's organized play time that focuses on a game or spe-cific activity. Observe how guys approach the game. Watch to see if they're all about the activity or just there to eat all the pizza! And see if they're innies or outies, sanguines or melancholies!

Second, there's simple hang time in coed settings that will give you different insights into Boylanders. What topics do they bring up—sports, school, girls, God? Out of the heart the mouth speaks! See how they handle various situations. Notice which qualities you admire in them.

Third, there are service-oriented activities to help put feet on your faith. These fall in line with our B.A.B.E. in Action activities in the other books in the B.A.B.E. Book series. God is thrilled when he sees his children using their time and energy for him. It also gives you a glimpse into a guy's levels of selfishness and genuine love for others.

So go use these special "craziness" times to just enjoy being with your friends from Boyland! ●

Becoming a B.A.B.E.

Everything about being a B.A.B.E. has to do with believing in God, having a personal relationship with his Son, Jesus Christ, by asking him to forgive your sin and come into your life and heart to be your saving Lord, and having his Holy Spirit actually living inside you. According to the Bible, that's when you become God's child, part of his forever family. As his child, you'll come to understand by reading the Bible that

> you're **beautiful** in God's eyes
>
> you're **accepted** unconditionally, without fear of rejection, by God
>
> you're **blessed** with spiritual gifts and special abilities
>
> you're **eternally significant** as you discover and live out the plan God has for your life

Beautiful, accepted, blessed, eternally significant! That makes you a B.A.B.E.!

It all starts with saying yes to God, yes to Jesus, yes to the Holy Spirit. If you've never done that, I invite you to pray a prayer something like this one:

Dear God,

I believe in you. I believe you created me and you love me. I believe you sent your Son, Jesus, to this earth to live a perfect life and then die on the cross for the sins of everyone—including me. Jesus, I ask you to forgive me for all the things I've done wrong. I invite you into my life to be the Savior of my sins and the Lord of my life. Please send your Holy Spirit, right now, to come live inside me. Let my body be his home. Now, Father God, show me my beauty through your eyes, teach me about how you value and accept me, and help me keep my focus on you and you alone. Help me identify and develop the spiritual gifts the Holy Spirit has just given me, and show me how to use my life in a way that makes a difference, a way that is eternally significant. I want to shine for you! In Jesus's name I pray. Amen!

Congrats! You've just become an official B.A.B.E.! Go tell someone! ●

You've been created *on* purpose and *for* a purpose.

CONFIRM YOUR B.A.B.E. STATUS!

Let's make it official. If you're ready to declare yourself a B.A.B.E.—now and forever—then sign on the dotted line. Make a copy of this page and send it along with a **self-addressed stamped envelope** (with $1.50 postage) to:

B.A.B.E. • P.O. Box 75 • Fort Myers, FL 33902

Your B.A.B.E. ID will be mailed directly to you.

I, _____, truly believe that I'm beautiful in my heavenly Father's eyes. I'm accepted by him unconditionally. I'm blessed with spiritual gifts and special abilities that he chose for me. I'm eternally significant with a life plan that will make a difference. I'm a B.A.B.E.

I choose to develop God-Beauty. I choose to have an audience of One and to see my value based upon what God's Word says about me. I choose to develop and use my gifts and talents for God's purposes. I choose to seek God's plan for my life so I'll be eternally significant and will bring him glory.

I choose to become the kind of young woman God can use. I choose to *be* the B.A.B.E. I am.

Signature: _____

Date: _____

Email: _____

Catch the
B.A.B.E. wave

Teen girls all over the globe are catching the B.A.B.E. wave! They're discovering that they're B.A.B.E.s in God's eyes, in his opinion, in his kingdom! And ultimately that's *all* that matters. Girls just like you want to honor God with their lives and live out his purposes for them.

The B.A.B.E. wave is on the move! And you can help keep it rolling.

Now that *you* understand that you're a B.A.B.E., you can help other girls discover that they too are beautiful, accepted, blessed, and eternally significant. You can skyrocket their self-esteem by chatting up the fact that they were created *on* purpose and *for* a purpose.

Wherever you live, whatever your life situation, you can start right now to shape your generation by giving them a crystal clear vision of who they are in Christ and what they're here on earth to do. Life isn't meaningless—not even sorta! Pray for opportunities to tell others—cousins, classmates, teammates, co-workers. Pray for the right words at the right time. Pray for listeners' hearts to be open. And pray for your B.A.B.E. girlfriends around the world to remember *who they are* and to be courageous, knowing that God is with them as they take this message to their peers.

Live the B.A.B.E. message. Share the B.A.B.E. message. Be the B.A.B.E. message. Keep the B.A.B.E. wave rolling.

I'll be praying for you! ●

Extra Stuff:
SPIRITUAL GIFTS LIST

The Bible tells us that God chooses at least one spiritual gift to give you—not exclusively, of course, but one you'll delight in using. Paul describes most of these gifts in Romans 12:6–8; 1 Corinthians 12:7–10, 28; and Ephesians 4:11–13. Read the definitions, then place a check mark by the gift(s) you may have.

Gifts in Romans

Prophecy: hearing a special "right now" message from God and speaking it to his people

Serving: recognizing jobs that need to be done and finding a way to complete them

Teaching: communicating information (by word and deed) so others can understand and grow

Exhortation: speaking words that encourage others and stimulate their faith

Giving: cheerfully and generously sharing what you have with others

Leading: catching God's vision, setting goals, and influencing others to help reach them

Mercy: genuinely feeling what others are feeling, then being sympathetic, comforting, and kind

Gifts in 1 Corinthians

Wisdom: using Holy Spirit–given insight to give wise advice right when it's needed

Knowledge: discovering, understanding, and clarifying information to help God's people

Faith: having unquenchable trust and confidence about God's plan and purposes

Healing: laying hands on ill people, praying for them, and seeing God cure them

Miracles: serving as the human instrument that receives God's power to perform powerful acts

Distinguishing of spirits: knowing if a person's spirit is of God or of Satan

Speaking in tongues: receiving and delivering a message from God through a divine language you've never learned; also used in private prayer to God

Interpreting tongues: receiving from God the translation of a message given in tongues

Prophecy: same as above

Gifts in Ephesians

Apostle: gathering believers together in a new environment

Evangelism: sharing the Good News of Jesus and winning nonbelievers to Christ

Pastoring: providing the care and spiritual feeding of God's people

Prophet and Teacher: described above

Gifts from Other Places in Scripture

Celibacy: remaining single and sexually abstinent for purposes of serving God (1 Corinthians 7:7)

Hospitality: welcoming into your home those who need food and/or lodging (1 Peter 4:9)

Intercession: praying on behalf of others; standing in the gap (Colossians 1:9–12)

Exorcism: casting out demons using God's supernatural power (Acts 16:16–18)

Helps: working behind the scenes to assist others in fulfilling their ministry (Romans 16:1–2)

Administration: creating a plan and organizing others to complete it (Titus 1:5)

Which spiritual gifts do you think you have?

_____

_____

_____

Which gifts do you see in your guy friends?

_____

_____

_____

The Boyland "Chat It Up"
GUIDE

When it comes to talking about guys, most of you B.A.B.E.s don't need a guide to get the conversation rolling. Just grab up a group of friends, read this book, and have fun blabbing about the topics it covers. You can get started by agreeing to read a section or a chapter—whatever works for you—for each time you meet. Each girl can come up with questions she wants to ask or topics she wants to discuss. (I know you won't have trouble coming up with your own question to discuss—that's why I'm not giving you any!)

Now agree on a time and place to meet up together and chat it up! You're going to have a blast with this one!

Suggestion: Your chat sessions will probably bring up some questions you and your friends can't really answer—other than your best educated guess. Take these questions to a woman you know and trust who can help you out. Don't settle for unanswered questions; it won't help you learn.

If you want to go through this book with a leader, pray about the best woman for the job and ask her. She'll be flattered. Then have her glance through the Boyland "Chat It Up" Leader's Guide on the next page. ●

The Boyland "Chat It Up"
Leader's Guide

I've personally witnessed the phenomenon that takes place when a group of girls gets together to talk (one of their favorite pastimes). Eventually their walls come down and their hearts open up. How special to be a part of that. And what B.A.B.E. doesn't like to talk about guys? It's great that you've chosen to be a part of this by being a leader!

Now you might be wondering what exactly your role as a group leader is. Here are some tips to get you started:

Andrea's Top Ten Guidelines for Leading a Chat Session

Here are some tips for enhancing your time with your group:

1. **Pray!** Pray for God's guidance as you prepare and share. Pray for each girl in your group. Pray that the eyes of her heart would be enlightened so she would know the hope of her calling (Ephesians 1:18). Pray that she would be filled with the knowledge of God's will in all spiritual wisdom and understanding so that she may walk in a manner worthy of the Lord, pleasing him in all areas of her life and bearing fruit in every good work she attempts for the Lord (Colossians 1:9–10). For those who don't know the Lord, pray that they would see their need for him and say yes to his saving grace.

2. **Be prepared!** Read through the entire book; then go back and prepare each week by reviewing the section and coming up with some questions and topics for discussion straight out of the text. For instance:

How does knowing the differences between a girl's brain and a guy's brain help you interpret a guy's answer to your questions or his reaction in a specific situation?

Who do you know who fits the melancholy personality type?

Why is hanging out in groups better than single dating?

Next week let's all experiment with conversation—choose a guy, then see if you can get from yes-or-no questions to open-ended questions.

Be willing to share one personal story that relates to the topic of the week, yet be sensitive to the amount of time you talk about you! One or two stories can help your group open up, but too many stories may make them feel you don't want to hear about them! Balance is always the key.

3. **Welcome them!** This works best when you're the first one to arrive at the meeting spot (church, Starbucks, a restaurant). Get some tunes going, mix up some lemonade, and be ready so that when they walk through the door, your attention is on them.

4. **Encourage participation!** The first few weeks, allow your group to participate at their own comfort level. Everyone need not answer every question. Eventually it will be good if each girl shares. After all, this book is all about guys and things girls deal with and things they have opinions on! For those shy

B.A.B.E.s, rather than just calling on them, which puts them on the spot, go for a gentler approach (instead of "Melissa, your turn," try "We'd love to hear how you answered that question, Melissa. Would you be willing to share?"). Now, for the girl who always has something to say and is the first one to say it, bring along some duct tape. Just kidding! Try something like, "Sarah, we like hearing your answers, but let's have someone else go first this time." Hopefully, that will help! **Important:** Every answer matters! No response is too insignificant. Do your best to validate and affirm their answers.

5. **Be genuine!** Ask questions with interest and warmth. Maintain as much eye contact with the group as possible (especially with the one who's talking). Be conscious of your facial expressions and body language (smiling is good; nodding off is bad).

6. **Go deeper!** If you want them to elaborate on an answer or you don't quite understand what they're saying, try phrases like, "Tell us more about that." "Why do you feel that way?" "How did that make you feel?" "What did you learn from that situation?" "What would you do differently next time?" "When you say _____, what does that mean to you?"

   With the subject matter in *Boyland*, you could elaborate by bringing in a few experts to chat with the girls (e.g., a counselor to talk about the importance of communication, STDs, or whatever). You could even bring in a panel of guys and let the girls shoot questions at them!

7. **Be creative!** Add visual aids like magazine ads, movie clips, props, posters, book excerpts, skits, role playing, and more!

Use your imagination. It keeps the learning fun for you and them!

8. **Let the Spirit lead!** Commit each week to the Lord. If the lesson seems to be going in a different direction or if your group seems intense on one aspect of the lesson, be willing to forgo the plan, trusting that the Spirit wants to do a work in the girls' lives right then. It's important to discern between the Holy Spirit's direction, a rabbit trail, and one girl getting on her soap box! But if there's sincere interaction, go with it. There might even be someone who becomes visibly upset or tearful. Feel free to stop to pray for her. Follow up by asking her if there's anything she needs or if there's anything you can do to help.

9. **Welcome silence!** I realize that five seconds can feel like five hours when you toss out a question and suddenly no one has a thing to say! Don't panic—allow them time to process the question and think about their answer. If necessary, reword the question and toss it out again.

10. **Be brave!** Two thoughts here. First, in a group of teen girls, there will be differences of opinion, levels of experience, and spiritual maturity. Allow for it and expect it. Do your best to highlight answers that are closest to the biblical point of view. Second, there are bound to be questions you can't answer. There may even be someone in the group who actually gets a kick out of trying to stump you! Believe me, I've been there. I encourage you to turn it into a positive and congratulate them for really thinking hard! It shows they're hungry for truth. Write down the question, and do your best to have an answer the next week. You might even challenge the group to search their Bibles ("What does the Bible say about wisdom?")

or poll girls at school ("What percentage of girls really think it's possible to be a virgin when they get married?") so that you can dig for the answer together.

Playing by the Rules!

Here are some simple rules to share with your small group:

Keep it confidential. What's shared in the group stays in the group.

Avoid judging. Respect the views of others.

Don't fix it. Offer advice only if it's requested.

No interrupting. Whoever's speaking, let her finish.

Take turns. Don't do all the talking. We learn more by listening.

Pray for group members. It's the kindest and most powerful thing you can do.

Getting Started!

Secure a copy of *Boyland* for each participant. Have pens/pencils, Bibles, and extra paper handy. Have a sign-in sheet—include name, address, phone number, and email address. Challenge yourself to memorize the girls' names ASAP. Personally contacting them a few times during the course of the study means the world to them. Send a note or an email or give them a call. If you have more than ten girls, recruit another leader and have two groups. You know your group best. Focus in on their needs.

Try This Lineup!

Hey, Glad You're Here! (greet them)

Get Those Pretty Little Heads Thinking! (general opening question)

Invite Jesus to Join You! (opening prayer)

What's God Up To? (praise reports/testimonies)

Hide It in Your Heart! (memory verse)

And the Answer Is . . . ! (Q & A)

Change and Rearrange! (personal application)

Wrap It Up! (closing prayer)

What's Up Next Week! (assignment and memory verse)

The Boyland Retreat Weekend

Want to mix it up a bit? Have a B.A.B.E.s-only retreat where the girls get to spill all weekend on their favorite topic—guys! Try one of these.

Option One: Give each girl a book and strongly suggest she read it before the retreat so she's prepared for the chat it up sessions.

Option Two: Give the girls the book when they arrive. Plan a schedule that includes specific preselected sections to read. Then gather together to chat.

Option Three: At the retreat, assign small groups to read certain sections. Then have them report on what they learned. ●

Don't miss other books in the
B.a.B.e. SERIES

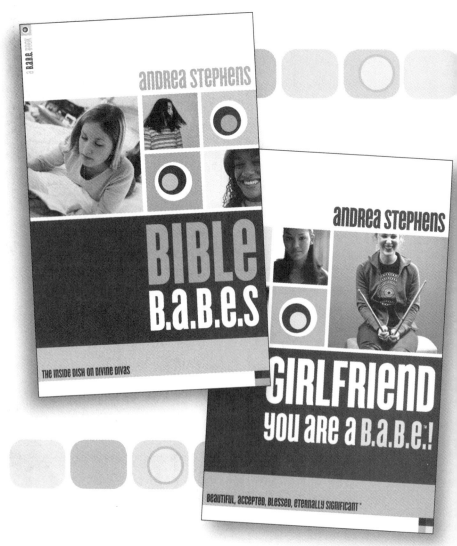

✳ ordinary girls doing extraordinary things

Brio magazine has the inside scoop on everything — boys, fitting in, parents, school, life! Every issue has tips on fashion, food, and friendship, as well as encouraging advice to ignite your faith. You'll find answers to questions about music and movies, plus inspiring articles about Christian entertainers and athletes. Subscribe today!

Request a subscription to *Brio* magazine for girls ages 12 to 16 or sign up for *Brio and Beyond* magazine for girls 16 and older by calling (800) A-FAMILY (232-6459) today.

In Canada, visit www.focusonthefamily.ca to learn about the ministry.

Wanna join *Brio* on a two-week international missions trip next summer? For details, go to www.briomag.com and click on "Brio Missions" or call (719) 548-4575 for more information.